TEACHER RESOURCES FOR THROWN TO THE WIND

2024 Edition

Amanda M. Cetas & Adriana R. King

Windy Sea Publishing, LLC | Tucson, Arizona

Teacher Resources for Thrown to the Wind

Windy Sea Publishing
Tucson, AZ
www.windyseapublishing.com

Second Edition, 2024
Copyright © 2020 First Edition
by Amanda M. Cetas
and Adriana R. King

All rights reserved. The authors grant the individual teacher permission to print copies of the student handouts from the Teacher Resource Book for use in their own classroom. This curriculum is licensed for single-teacher use only. Duplication of this document for the purpose of resale or other distribution is prohibited. Permission is not granted to post this document for use online. This curriculum is protected by copyright. Contact us for permission to use any of this material in any other manner than stipulated above.

ISBN-13: 978-1-7332034-6-3 Ingram
ISBN-13: 978-1-7332034-7-0 Amazon
ISBN-13: 978-1-956277-26-5 PDF

Editor: Fantastic Literary Services, LLC

Cover Design: A. Marie Hanson

Jacket Images:
Map: 1814 Thomson Map of the Atlantic Ocean, Public Domain
Novel cover design by nskvsky

Table of Contents

Note to Teachers   **Page 1**
Notes on the period, teaching methods, adapting them to the individual classroom, assessing student achievement, and cross-curricular opportunities.

Concept Maps   **Page 3**
Includes a brief description of each chapter in the book, essential questions, vocabulary words, national standards, and additional information.

Part 1, The Flight   **Page 14**
1. Teacher's Overview
2. Bell Ringer
3. Part 1, Historical summary
    a. Scaffolded Annotation Student Worksheet
    b. Non-scaffolded Historical Summary
    c. Discussion Questions
4. Discussion Questions by Chapter
5. *The Log of a Cabin Boy*
   This is a non-fiction memoir account of a boy who makes a life for himself by taking to sea as a cabin boy. (See Additional Resources.)
    a. Discussion Questions
    b. Comparative Essay Prompt
6. Constellation Project
   Create their own constellation and write a short myth to explain it.

Part 2, Refugees   **Page 38**
1. Teacher's Overview
2. Bell Ringer
3. Part 2, Historical summary
    a. Scaffolded Annotation Student Worksheet
    b. Non-scaffolded Historical Summary
    c. Discussion Questions
    d. Research Project (with Teacher Instructions)
       Students (individually or in small groups) will research one of the topics listed in the historical summary to become "experts" and share with the rest of the class.
    e. Argumentative Essay
4. Discussion Questions by Chapter
5. Essay/Story Rewrite
   Develop a cause and effect timeline; then, rewrite the story changing one decision and exploring how that would affect the outcome.
6. Trade Route Assignments
    a. Persuasive Letter
       Write a letter to a wealthy merchant asking to patronize their voyage.
    b. Adventure Journal Assignment
       Write journal entries to describe the New World and experiences on the adventure.
7. Trade Game/Simulation – **Available for download** at http://www.amandamcetas.com.
   Students will explore the complex world of the 17th century in this fun choose-your-own-adventure game.
8. Persuasive Essay Prompt

Part 3, The Voyage   **Page 76**
1. Teacher's Overview
2. Bell Ringer
3. Part 3 Historical Summary
    a. Non-scaffolded Historical Summary
    b. Research Project (with Teacher Instructions)
       Students (individually or in small groups) will research one of the nautical discoveries listed in the historical summary and demonstrate its use to the class.
    c. Women Pirates Viewer's Guide
4. Discussion Questions by Chapter
5. Analytical Essay
6. Map Project
   Create and describe a fictitious Huguenot family and chart their path to safety.

Part 4, A New World   **Page 95**
1. Teacher's Overview
2. Bell Ringer
3. Part 4, Historical Summary
    a. Non-scaffolded Historical Summary
    b. Discussion Questions
4. Discussion Questions by Chapter
5. Essay Idea List
6. Wrap-up Project List

Appendices   **Page 104**
A. Checklists and Rubrics
B. Additional Sources
C. Sources Cited

About the Authors

Amanda M. Cetas is the author of the historical adventure **Thrown to the Wind**, which is the first book in the series, *A Country for Castoffs*. The story is taken from her family history, which she has spent over two decades researching. She currently teaches several courses in American, European and World history to advanced high school students. She also taught at the middle school level for several years.

Adriana R. King has been passionate about the art of story telling her whole life, but it wasn't until college in NYC that she discovered the depth and beauty of a story well-told. She also studied abroad at Oxford University. There she learned that every literary technique carries its own value in a story. After college, she spent 3 years as an English teacher where she provided individualized writing feedback and discovered that editing makes our minds stronger and our writing more intentional.

Note to Teachers

The period of the Religious Wars in Europe is often a difficult one to teach, and teaching resources to support student learning in this area has been limited. This period is, however, an important one in European and American history, because it is foundational to explaining the many political conflicts and trade wars between various European countries and their colonies. It was the impetus for many groups of people coming to settle in North America. It set the stage for the development of the founding principles of the United States, especially the First Amendment to the U.S. Constitution.

This guide is designed to provide teachers with resources they can use to help their students understand this period through engaging activities, varied learning opportunities, and utilizes both formative and summative assessment methods. Suggestions are provided about how to adapt these resources to your classroom. The resources provided here were developed from years of experience in teaching and educational research on student-centered instruction.

Adjusting for Students with Differing Abilities

Teachers of students at all levels – from middle school to high school – can use these materials successfully. Some of the materials have already been scaffolded, such as some of the historical summaries. Teachers can also use the materials in different ways or make adjustments to address their teaching style and the needs of their students. Here are some suggestions:

- Use the Bell Ringers to introduce the topics discussed in each section of the reading.
- Read some sections of the readings out loud.
- Break up the readings into shorter chunks.
- Preview the vocabulary and key concepts listed in the Concept Maps. Establish a system to help students find the definitions and use the words in context.
- Use images to associate with difficult or unfamiliar vocabulary words.
- The discussion questions can be done individually by students or in small groups. They can be written or discussed orally or written and then discussed either in small groups or in large class discussions. It has been shown that giving students a chance to read and answer questions, and then to discuss their answers in small groups, before sharing with the class, can help to build student confidence in class discussions/activities.
- The projects and simulations also provide opportunities to group students in different ways and provide opportunities for students to demonstrate their knowledge in different ways to highlight their unique strengths and abilities while holding everyone in the group responsible for their contributions.
- Create a Know/Want to Know/Learned (K-W-L) worksheet for students to record what they already know about the Reformation and Religious Wars and what they would like to learn about them. Then as they read, have them complete the "learned" section of the worksheet.
- Brainstorm students' current knowledge and create a class web or graphic organizer to connect their ideas about the topics.
- Ask students to complete their own graphic organizers for sections of the reading individually or in pairs.

Assessing Student Achievement

Numerous tools for assessing, including rubrics, are available throughout this guide and in Appendix A.

Grading Group Assignments: Group work can be motivating for students, but it can also be a source of conflict. To mitigate some of this conflict, keep groups small, ideally no more than three to four students to a group. Each student should have their own area of responsibility. For larger classes, five in a group can work, but it is even more important to have designated assignments, that are known to everyone in the group and the teacher. It can also be helpful to have students within the group assess the effectiveness of their group, as well as their own performance, at the end.

Testing: The activities in this resource have been designed to teach students to think critically, analyze multiple perspectives, and articulate individual conclusions. Essay prompts have been provided to help students demonstrate critical thinking and historical understanding. These can also be modified into short answer responses depending on student abilities. In some cases, teachers may opt to provide a single prompt or assessment to the class, or the teacher may choose to provide several choices from which students may select from a list of prompts or assessments.

Cross-Curricular Opportunities

While the bulk of the methods in this resource are designed for English Language Arts courses, many of the activities, projects, and simulations can be integrated into a variety of courses or used effectively in a cross-curricular program.

Literature: This unit provides opportunities to explore narrative in historical fiction and to compare it to informational texts. Additionally, the Constellation Project connects with Nordic and Greco-Roman mythologies and provides opportunities for students to create their own constellations and mythological stories. Various assessments are provided to allow students to practice writing argumentative, informative, and narrative essays.

Social Studies: This unit provides historical background information on the Reformation and Wars of Religion, including the Siege of La Rochelle and the rise of King Louis XIV of France. Students are also given the opportunity to compare and contrast 17th-century French society, government, and economics with that of the Dutch Republic. Also provided is a timeline of European exploration and colonization of North America to set the stage for learning United States History.

STEM: This unit provides opportunities to learn about early understandings of astronomy through the study of constellations. Additionally, a research project is provided to teach students about the development of navigational discoveries and inventions, which will also help students develops presentation skills. Finally, a Mapping Project will introduce students to principals of cartography, while also tapping into their creativity and imagination.

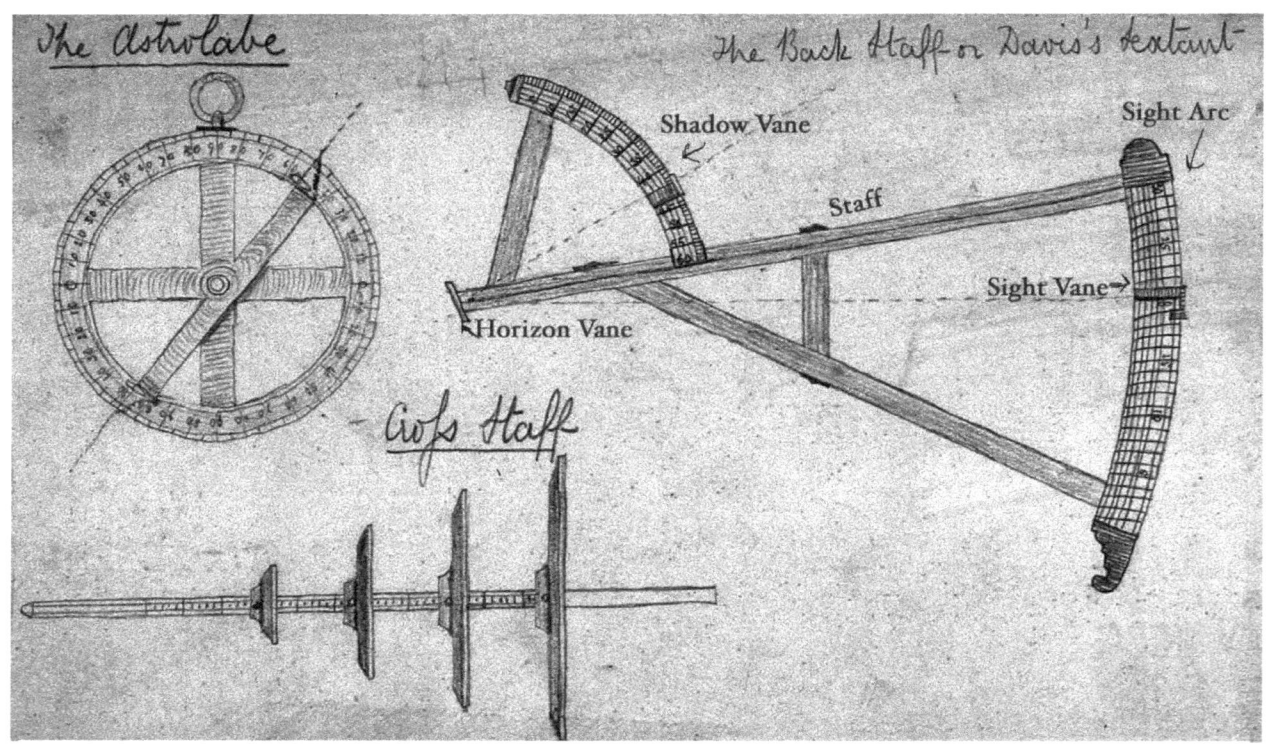

Navigation: An Astrolabe, a Cross-staff, and a Back-staff or Davis's Sextant.
Drawing after Edmund Gunter, 1624.
Black & white and labeled. Welcome Collection
Creative Commons Attribution only license CC BY 4.0
http://creativecommons.org/licenses/by/4.0/

Concept Map

Concept Map of Thrown to the Wind: Part 1: The Flight

Etienne is faced with a difficult choice: Does he flee La Rochelle, France with his family and become another Huguenot on the run, or does he stay and hide out with his cousin, converting to Catholicism, so that he can pursue his dream of becoming a musketeer?

KEY LEARNING(S)		UNIT ESSENTIAL QUESTIONS	OPTIONAL INSTRUCTION TOOLS
PICTURE ANALYSIS	**PART 1 HISTORICAL SUMMARY**	**CHAPTER 1**	**CHAPTER 2**
La Rochelle, The Harbour Entrance, *by Jean Baptist Camille Corot*, The Yorck Project (2002)	History of the Religious Persecution in France.	Trouble is brewing in La Rochelle, France. Etienne secretly meets with his cousin and closest friend, Nicolas, who warns him about the escalating tensions between the Protestants and Catholics.	Etienne gets a taste of what it would be like to be a musketeer and hears a new perspective.
ESSENTIAL QUESTIONS	**ESSENTIAL QUESTIONS**	**ESSENTIAL QUESTIONS**	**ESSENTIAL QUESTIONS**
1. What purposes do the towers serve in this image? Why do you think this city would build towers like these on either side of the mouth to the inner harbor? 2. What else can you learn about this city, based on the visual elements present in the image? 3. Would you want to live in this city? Why or why not?	1. What is the writer's purpose for writing? Does the writer display any bias? 2. Identify and organize the major historical events described. 3. Who were the most significant people, events, or policies in the War of Religions? Why were they important? 4. Have the Wars of Religion caused any lasting effects in today's society? 5. How did the conflict between the Roman Catholics and Protestants unify and/or divide Europe?	1. What details does the author use to create a sense of urgency, unease, and/or tension? 2. Who is the narrator? How would you describe him? 3. What is the setting? Where does it fit in with the historical summary? How does the novel setting compare to the historical context? 4. How can context and connotation help to define unexplained French terms in the story? 5. What is important about the title "Musketeers"? What does it imply?	1. How do the protestant and catholic arguments about the Siege of La Rochelle compare and contrast? How does the author's explanations line up with the historical summary? 2. Based on context and connotation, what is a "maître" and what is its significance to the text. 3. What is a musketeer and why are there so many in the city? What value does Etienne's encounter with one bring to the story?
VOCABULARY	**VOCABULARY**	**VOCABULARY**	**VOCABULARY**
	<u>With Annotation Guide</u> – Use the annotation guide to identify unknown or important words. <u>Without Annotation Guide</u> - Underline all the words that appear to be technical history terms (Scaffolded: Use the highlighted words). Use the context around the word to create a guess definition then look up the word in the dictionary.	Huguenots Conspiratorially Heresy Judicial Municipal	Papist Mandates Petition Cyphering Catechism Edict Magnanimous Tolerance
COMMON CORE STANDARDS	**COMMON CORE STANDARDS**	**COMMON CORE STANDARDS**	**COMMON CORE STANDARDS**
	CCSS.ELA-LITERACY.RH.7.1-6, 7	CCSS.ELA-Literacy.RL.7.1-7, 9; L.7.1-5	CCSS.ELA-Literacy.RL.7.1-7, 9; L.7.1-5
ADDITIONAL INFORMATION			

Thrown to the Wind Teacher's Resource   *Windy Sea Publishing, LLC*   www.windyseapublishing.com

Concept Map of Thrown to the Wind: Part 1: The Flight

Etienne is faced with a difficult choice: Does he flee La Rochelle, France with his family and become another Huguenot on the run, or does he stay and hide out with his cousin, converting to Catholicism, so that he can pursue his dream of becoming a musketeer?

KEY LEARNING(S)		UNIT ESSENTIAL QUESTIONS	OPTIONAL INSTRUCTION TOOLS
CHAPTERS 3-4	**CHAPTERS 5-8**	**CHAPTER 9**	**CHAPTER 10**
Etienne must make a hard decision and only time will tell if it was the right one.	Etienne and his family board a ship in order to flee the country but danger is still lurking around the corner.	Etienne is hoodwinked and comes face to face with the circumstances around his brother's death.	A new door opens to Etienne. Has he finally found his calling?
ESSENTIAL QUESTIONS	**ESSENTIAL QUESTIONS**	**ESSENTIAL QUESTIONS**	**ESSENTIAL QUESTIONS**
1. How does Etienne Sr's use of language reflect on his relationship with Etienne Jr? 2. How does the author use the biblical story of Daniel and the lion's den as a foreshadowing technique? What are some other reasons the author might have had when she included this analogy in her story? 3. What are Etienne's motivations and what reasons does he give to support them?	1. How does the author use symbolism in Chapter 5? 2. What are the motivations behind Etienne's actions and how would the story be different had he made a different decision? 3. Using textual evidence, how would you assess the actions of the officer? 4. How do the Protestant and Catholic perspectives compare and contrast? 5. Is Etienne an active or passive character?	1. How does the historical context shape Etienne's actions and his relationships with others? 2. Is Etienne responsible for his brother's death? Why or why not? 3. Why does the author use a flashback in this chapter? How does it bring value to the plot and/or character development of the story?	1. When confronted by the captain, why does Etienne not tell on Francois and his friends? 2. How does Etienne start to take his life into his own hands? What motivates him to do so? 3. How would you describe Etienne's character? Did he make the right decision in asking to become a cabin boy, or not? Why or why not?
VOCABULARY	**VOCABULARY**	**VOCABULARY**	**VOCABULARY**
Endearment Incomprehensible Christening Allegedly Disavow Calvinists Pungent	Curfew Obsidian Rhythmic Compliance Ballast Channel Doctrine Infallible Blasphemy	Tumultuous Pretense Prole Mourning Posse Dependable	Leverage Involuntarily Quizzically Gaunt Sponsor
COMMON CORE STANDARDS	**COMMON CORE STANDARDS**	**COMMON CORE STANDARDS**	**COMMON CORE STANDARDS**
CCSS.ELA-Literacy.RL.7.1-7, 9; L.7.1-5	CCSS.ELA-Literacy.RL.7.1-7, 9; L.7.1-5	CCSS.ELA-Literacy.RL.7.1-7, 9; L.7.1-5	CCSS.ELA-Literacy.RL.7.1-7, 9; L.7.1-5

ADDITIONAL INFORMATION

Concept Map of Thrown to the Wind: Part 1: The Flight

Etienne is faced with a difficult choice: Does he flee La Rochelle, France with his family and become another Huguenot on the run, or does he stay and hide out with his cousin, converting to Catholicism, so that he can pursue his dream of becoming a musketeer?

KEY LEARNING(S)		UNIT ESSENTIAL QUESTIONS	OPTIONAL INSTRUCTION TOOLS
CHAPTER 11	**CHAPTER 12-13**	**THE LOG OF A CABIN BOY**	**CONSTELLATION PROJECT**
Etienne learns a lot in his new position as cabin boy.	Etienne has another confrontation with Francois and their ship makes port in Texel just outside of New Amsterdam.	This is a story of a boy who makes a life for himself by taking to the sea as a cabin boy.	Students will create their own constellation and write a short myth to explain it.
ESSENTIAL QUESTIONS	**ESSENTIAL QUESTIONS**	**ESSENTIAL QUESTIONS**	**LEARNING OBJECTIVES**
1. What does Etienne learn in this chapter and how might these skills help him (literally or metaphorically) later in the story? 2. What might the knot tying lesson be foreshadowing? 3. Identify some unexplained ship names. How do you think these terms got their names? 4. Why did people connect stars into images and create stories around them? What does this say about human nature? 5. What does Etienne learn when he talks to Captain Carteret about the death of the captain's nephew? How does this scene relate to Etienne?	1. What distinguishes adulthood from childhood? How does this reflect on Etienne? 2. What is Etienne Sr.'s relationship to the captain and what does his body language in this scene say about his character? 3. Evaluate Etienne's relationship with his father. Was it fair of Etienne's father to reject the captain's offer? How might this change Etienne's relationship with his father?	1. What is the purpose and bias of this text? 2. How do the pictures/sketches bring value to the story? 3. What kinds of duties were cabin boys expected to perform according to this text? **Essay Prompt:** Compare and contrast Etienne's story with that of Max Schmidt. How are their stories similar? How are they different? Based on the similarities and differences, make a prediction about what you think will happen in Etienne's story. Use textual evidence from both sources to support your answer.	1. Understand the thought process behind sailors creating constellations. 2. Create your own constellation and accompanying mythology. 3. Use narrative techniques to write a captivating story.
VOCABULARY	**VOCABULARY**	**VOCABULARY**	**VOCABULARY**
Rigging Constellations Accost Consoled Predicament Eerily Liberating Unsupervised Unruliness Insubordination	Computations Ridicule Demeanor Jibing Evident Diligently Integrity Nautical Disembark Midshipman		
COMMON CORE STANDARDS	**COMMON CORE STANDARDS**	**COMMON CORE STANDARDS**	**COMMON CORE STANDARDS**
CCSS.ELA-Literacy.RL.7.1-7, 9; L.7.1-5	CCSS.ELA-Literacy.RL.7.1-7, 9; L.7.1-5	CCSS.ELA-Literacy.RL.7.1-7, 9; W.7.2a-f, 4-6; L.7.1-5	CCSS.ELA-Literacy.SL.7.1a-d, 4-6; L.7.1-3

ADDITIONAL INFORMATION

The Log of a Cabin Boy: Available as a pdf free of charge at Google Books, see link in Appendix B.

Thrown to the Wind Teacher's Resource   *Windy Sea Publishing, LLC*   www.windyseapublishing.com

Concept Map of Thrown to the Wind: Part 2: Refugees

Etienne and his family arrive in New Amsterdam where new challenges and dangers arise.

KEY LEARNING(S)	UNIT ESSENTIAL QUESTIONS		OPTIONAL INSTRUCTION TOOLS
PICTURE ANALYSIS	**PART 2 HISTORICAL SUMMARY**	**RESEARCH PROJECT**	**ARGUMENTATIVE ESSAY**
Return to Amsterdam of the Second Expedition to the East Indies (1599), by Hendrick Cornelisz Vroom, Rijksmuseum, Amsterdam	A comparative look at the cultures, governments, and economies of France and Amsterdam.	Students will use the historical summary as well as external research to become "experts" on one of the topics in the historical summary, and then teach others what they learned.	Students will write an argumentative essay about whether it would have been better to live in France or New Amsterdam.
ESSENTIAL QUESTIONS	**ESSENTIAL QUESTIONS**	**ESSENTIAL QUESTIONS**	**Essay Prompt**
1. How many different types of ships are there in this image? Describe the characteristics of the different types of ships? 2. Based on your answer above, what can you infer about Texel Harbor? For example, in what ways do people make their living? How successful are they? 3. What is the point of view portrayed in the image? Does the artist have a favorable or negative view of the activity in the harbor? What evidence or visual features support your conclusion?	1. What are the most significant differences between the 17th century countries of France and New Netherlands? 2. What are the most significant similarities? 3. How did the Huguenot immigration/emigration change or affect each country? 4. What role did religion play in both countries?	1. What are the most significant differences between the 17th century countries of France and New Netherlands? 2. What are the most significant similarities? 3. How did the Huguenot immigration/emigration change or affect each country? 4. What role did religion play in both countries?	Compare and contrast the 17th century countries of France and New Netherlands. Then write and argumentative essay explaining which country would be best to live in and why.
VOCABULARY	**VOCABULARY**	**VOCABULARY**	**VOCABULARY**
	<u>With Annotation Guide</u> – Use the annotation guide to identify unknown or important words. <u>Without Annotation Guide</u> - Underline all the words that appear to be technical history terms (Scaffolded: Use the highlighted words). Use the context around the word to create a guess definition then look up the word in the dictionary.		
COMMON CORE STANDARDS	**COMMON CORE STANDARDS** CCSS.ELA-LITERACY.RH.7.1-6, 7	**COMMON CORE STANDARDS** CCSS.ELA-Literacy.W.7.1-2, 4-9; RI/RL.7.1-4; SL.7.1-5, 6; L.7.1-5	**COMMON CORE STANDARDS** CCSS.ELA-Literacy.W.7.1a-e, 4-6; L.7.1-5

ADDITIONAL INFORMATION

Richard's Dystopian Pokeverse site includes images of an amazing diorama of Texel Harbor in the 17th century and is referenced in Appendix B.

Concept Map of Thrown to the Wind: Part 2: Refugees

Etienne and his family arrive in New Amsterdam where new challenges and dangers arise.

KEY LEARNING(S)	UNIT ESSENTIAL QUESTIONS		OPTIONAL INSTRUCTION TOOLS
CHAPTERS 14-16	**CHAPTERS 17-19**	**CHAPTERS 20-21**	**CHAPTER 22**
Etienne and his family make it to New Amsterdam, but disaster strikes almost immediately.	Etienne finds his father wounded and robbed. He must now find a way to provide for the family.	Etienne and his family are now in the service of the mysterious Mr. Janssen van de Burgh.	Etienne finds himself in hot water.

ESSENTIAL QUESTIONS (Chapters 14-16)
1. How does the author reestablish the setting? What details does she focus on and how do these details add value to the story?
2. How does the author's representation of New Amsterdam compare and contrast with the historical summary?
3. What techniques does the author use to create suspense?

ESSENTIAL QUESTIONS (Chapters 17-19)
1. How does Etienne react when he finds his father? What does this new plot point add or contribute to the story as a whole as well as to Etienne's character development?
2. How would you assess Etienne's decisions since taking charge of the family? Did he make the right choices, or not? Explain.

ESSENTIAL QUESTIONS (Chapters 20-21)
1. How has Etienne's character developed since the start of the book?
2. What new relationships has Etienne developed? How do they compare to the relationships he had back in France?

ESSENTIAL QUESTIONS (Chapter 22)
1. How did Etienne end up being shanghaied aboard the *Sinjoor*?
2. Who does Etienne blame for his situation and is he justified in his blame?
3. What is the significance of the promise he makes?

VOCABULARY	VOCABULARY	VOCABULARY	VOCABULARY
Insignia	Poultice	Torrent	Shrubbery
Radial	Hospice	Barrage	Permeated
Quays	Ominous	Mortar	Corsairs
Guttural	Imposing	Harpsichord	Moorings
Couche	Requisitions	Burgermeister	Protruding
Artisans	Nefarious	Exorbitant	Burly
Affluent	Flustered	Vibrant	
Bourgeoisie	Indentured Servitude	Unsuitable	
Tantalizing	Brutish		
Almshouse	Lucrative		

COMMON CORE STANDARDS	COMMON CORE STANDARDS	COMMON CORE STANDARDS	COMMON CORE STANDARDS
CCSS.ELA-Literacy.RL.7.1-7, 9; L.7.1-5	CCSS.ELA-Literacy.RL.7.1-7, 9; L.7.1-5	CCSS.ELA-Literacy.RL.7.1-7, 9; L.7.1-5	CCSS.ELA-Literacy.RL.7.1-7, 9; L.7.1-5

ADDITIONAL INFORMATION

Student Reading Assessment Project: Have students develop a timeline to evaluate the causes and effects of Etienne's actions for chapters 17-24.

Images on French stoves, *Les Potagers*, are available on Marcus Flynn's site at http://www.pyromasse.ca/articles/potager_e.html.

Concept Map of Thrown to the Wind: Part 2: Refugees

Etienne and his family arrive in New Amsterdam where new challenges and dangers arise.

KEY LEARNING(S)	UNIT ESSENTIAL QUESTIONS		OPTIONAL INSTRUCTION TOOLS
CHAPTERS 23-24 Etienne is "baptized."	**ESSAY/STORY REWRITE** Using their cause and effect timelines, students will rewrite the story, changing one important cause or effect from the story.	**GAME/PROJECT*** Students will explore the complex trade world of the 17th century in this fun choose your own adventure game.	**PERSAUSIVE LETTER** Prior to the start of the game, the teacher has the option to assign this persuasive letter assignment where students will write a letter trying to convince a wealthy merchant to patronize their sea voyage.
ESSENTIAL QUESTIONS 1. Was is the significance of the title "Baptism?" What does the baptism in this chapter symbolize? 2. What are the consequences of Etienne's actions in these two chapters? 3. In Chapter 24, how does the author use everyday items to communicate/ symbolize complex emotions/ideas?	**ESSENTIAL QUESTIONS/ OBJECTIVES** 1. Using the action and effect timeline, rewrite the story changing AT LEAST one action or effect. 2. How would it change the story if Etienne made a different decision or if things played out differently? 3. Rewrite the scene using Etienne's point of view and make sure the story still flows naturally and believably.	**LEARNING OBJECTIVES** 1. Students will learn about the international trade between Europe and the Americas. 2. Students will learn about the many dangers of ocean travel. 3. Students will experience how social class in New Amsterdam was connected to wealth. 4. Students will explore cause and effect.	**Essay Prompt** Write a persuasive letter convincing a wealthy merchant or aristocrat to sponsor your journey to the New World. Focus on all the good your journey will do and explain the precautions you plan to take in order to ensure that you have a smooth journey despite all the dangers. Make sure to provide a reason that your voyage would benefit them.
VOCABULARY Whittled Perimeter Acutely Interminable Imperceptibly Somber Withdrawn Confiscated	**VOCABULARY**	**VOCABULARY**	**VOCABULARY**
COMMON CORE STANDARDS CCSS.ELA-Literacy.RL.7.1-7, 9; L.7.1-5	**COMMON CORE STANDARDS** CCSS.ELA-Literacy.W.7.3a-e, 4-6; L.7.1-5	**COMMON CORE STANDARDS** CCSS.ELA-Literacy.SL.7.1a-d, 4-6; L.7.1-3	**COMMON CORE STANDARDS** CCSS.ELA-Literacy.W.7.1a-e, 4-6; L.7.1-5

ADDITIONAL INFORMATION

* The Trade Route Game will be printed in a separate booklet, included along with this resource, or for free download at www.amandamcetas.com.

Concept Map of Thrown to the Wind: Part 2: Refugees

Etienne and his family arrive in New Amsterdam where new challenges and dangers arise.

KEY LEARNING(S)	UNIT ESSENTIAL QUESTIONS	OPTIONAL INSTRUCTION TOOLS

ADVENTURE JOURNAL

During phase 2 of the game or as a stand-alone assignment, the teacher has the option to assign this adventure journal assignment where students will write a short story (in the form of journal entries) about their character's adventures in the New World.

LEARNING OBJECTIVES

1. Imagine this is your first time in a new land that geographically is very different than what you have seen before.
2. Write an adventure journal describing this new land and your adventures in it. Be sure to use lots of sensory details and imagery in order to really capture the setting. Make sure to include ALL five senses in your description.

VOCABULARY

COMMON CORE STANDARDS

CCSS.ELA-Literacy.W.7.3a-e, 4-6; L.7.1-5

ADDITIONAL INFORMATION

Concept Map of Thrown to the Wind: Part 3: The Voyage

Etienne and his family are on the run again, sailing to the New World, where they can only hope things will be better.

KEY LEARNING(S)	UNIT ESSENTIAL QUESTIONS		OPTIONAL INSTRUCTION TOOLS
PICTURE ANALYSIS	**PART 3 HISTORICAL SUMMARY**	**RESEARCH PROJECT**	**CHAPTERS 25-27**
De Vergulde Bever (The Gilded Beaver) (1660), by Hendrick Cornelisz Vroom, Rijksmuseum, Amsterdam	History of nautical discoveries.	Students, individually or in groups, will be responsible for researching one of the nautical discoveries listed in the historical summary and demonstrate its use to the class.	Francois and Etienne come to blows and danger strikes from above.
ESSENTIAL QUESTIONS	**ESSENTIAL QUESTIONS**	**ESSENTIAL QUESTIONS**	**ESSENTIAL QUESTIONS**
1. What technological developments would a ship like this need in order to cross the Atlantic Ocean? 2. Based on the visual elements in the image, what is the purpose of this ship? Explain your answer by referencing specific evidence. 3. What kinds of supplies would be needed to survive a trip across the ocean? Of the supplies you listed, which would be the most important? Why?	1. When and how was the item/technology discovered? 2. How is it used and why does it work? 3. How successful was it and/or what other inventions were inspired by it?	1. When and how was the item/technology discovered? 2. How is it used and why does it work? 3. How successful was it and/or what other inventions were inspired by it?	1. Analyze Francois motivations and his behavior toward Etienne. Assess their relationship and how it has changed. 2. Compare and contrast Etienne with the new character Jan. How are they similar and how are they different? 3. Why does the author include the biblical analogy of Jonah and the whale? What is the significance of this analogy? How does it relate to Etienne?
VOCABULARY	**VOCABULARY**	**VOCABULARY**	**VOCABULARY**
			Faring Commandeering Aptitude Lashed Confinement Latrines Taunt Presumably Infernal Sentiments
COMMON CORE STANDARDS	**COMMON CORE STANDARDS** CCSS.ELA-LITERACY.RH.7.1-6, 7	**COMMON CORE STANDARDS**	**COMMON CORE STANDARDS** CCSS.ELA-Literacy.RL.7.1-7, 9; L.7.1-5

ADDITIONAL INFORMATION

Navigational information for teachers and students and numerous student activities for creating and using early navigational tools are referenced in Appendix B.

Concept Map of Thrown to the Wind: Part 3: The Voyage

Etienne and his family are on the run again, sailing to the New World, where they can only hope things will be better.

KEY LEARNING(S)	UNIT ESSENTIAL QUESTIONS	OPTIONAL INSTRUCTION TOOLS
CHAPTER 28-30 Etienne saves another Lefevre brother and there is a scurvy outbreak on the Gilded Beaver.	**ANALYSIS ESSAY** Students will evaluate and analysis Etienne's character growth throughout the novel so far.	**PROJECT** Students will create and describe a fictitious Huguenot family and have to chart their path to safety.
ESSENTIAL QUESTIONS 1. How do François and Tomas compare and contrast? Why are their reactions to Etienne so different? 2. How has Etienne grown or changed throughout the novel? 3. In chapter 30, Lidie claims to have seen their dead brother, Louis. What is the significance of this scene?	**ESSENTIAL QUESTIONS** 1. How has Etienne grown or developed over the course of the novel? 2. Captain Carteret once said that the difference between an adult and a child was that an adult stood by his/her word. According to this definition, would you describe Etienne as a child or an adult? Explain your answer and use textual evidence to support it.	**LEARNING OBJECTIVES** 1. Students will learn about the many other possible routes out of France as well as the possible dangers each presented. 2. Students will research the effects of the protestant migration. 3. Students will create and develop their own characters and map their journeys out of France.
VOCABULARY Ominous Corsairs Ironically Detained Adjourned Impending Palpable Commotion Erupted Cauterized	**VOCABULARY**	**VOCABULARY**
COMMON CORE STANDARDS CCSS.ELA-Literacy.RL.7.1-7, 9; L.7.1-5	**COMMON CORE STANDARDS** CCSS.ELA-Literacy.W.7.1a-e, 4-6; L.7.1-5	**COMMON CORE STANDARDS** CCSS.ELA-Literacy.SL.7.1a-d, 4-6; L.7.1-3

ADDITIONAL INFORMATION

The English translation of the journal of *De Bever* is available from the Vanderhoof Family History Project and is referenced in Appendix B.

Concept Map of Thrown to the Wind: Part 4: A New World

Can Etienne save his sister in time? What will his and his family's lives be like in this new and strange land.

KEY LEARNING(S)		UNIT ESSENTIAL QUESTIONS	OPTIONAL INSTRUCTION TOOLS
PICTURE ANALYSIS	**PART 4 HISTORICAL SUMMARY**	**CHAPTERS 31-EPILOGUE**	**SUMMATIVE ASSESSEMENT**
A view of New Amsterdam from Governor's Island, Manhattan 1660, by Len Tantillo.	A brief historical summary of the New World.	Etienne's sister has contracted scurvy, but the only way to save her is to disobey everyone and sneak his way off the ship. Will he be able to make it back in time?	The teacher or students will choose a wrap-up essay from the list provided.
ESSENTIAL QUESTIONS	**ESSENTIAL QUESTIONS**	**ESSENTIAL QUESTIONS**	**ESSAY PROMPTS**
1. What technological developments would a ship like this need in order to cross the Atlantic Ocean? 2. Based on the visual elements in the image, what is the purpose of this ship? Explain your answer by referencing specific evidence. 3. What kinds of supplies would be needed to survive a trip across the ocean? Of the supplies you listed, which would be the most important? Why?	1. Why did the Dutch wish to establish a colony in North America? What did they hope to gain? 2. How can the relationship between the Native Americans and the colonies be described? 3. In what ways did the Native Americans benefit from their associations with the colonist? In what ways were they harmed by these associations?	1. How does the author establish the new setting? 2. Is Etienne an active or passive character and how does this compare to what he was like at the beginning of the book? 3. What is the significance of the old beggar woman? 4. Why is the introduction of the character Alsoomse significant? Compare and contrast her to the other characters Etienne meets in the New World. 5. Why is the last chapter titled, "forgiveness"? 6. What value does the epilogue bring to the story?	1. How did Etienne's mother change throughout the story? While she appears to be a small character, why is she so important to the story? In what ways did she help drive the story forward? 2. Trace and evaluate Etienne and Francois' relationship. Why was this relationship so important to the story? How does it reflect Etienne's character growth? 3. Is disobedience for a good cause justified? Why or why not? How would Etienne answer this question? How might Etienne's father answer it? His mother? How would the author answer it? 4. How might Etienne's story connect to immigration problems today? Is there a connection? What are some similarities? What are some differences? What lessons about immigration can we learn from Etienne? 5. Why was there so much animosity between the Protestants and Catholics? How does the religious persecution in the book and in history relate to today? Do we see the same issues in our society? What does this say about humanity? What should be our response to differing belief systems?
VOCABULARY	**VOCABULARY**	**VOCABULARY**	
		Discernibly Decorum Ebony Constable Magistrate Stockade Quarantined Debauched Lintels Dappled	
COMMON CORE STANDARDS	**COMMON CORE STANDARDS**	**COMMON CORE STANDARDS**	**COMMON CORE STANDARDS**
	CCSS.ELA-LITERACY.RH.7.1-6, 7	**CCSS.ELA-Literacy.**RL.7.1-7, 9; L.7.1-5	**CCSS.ELA-Literacy.**W.7.1a-e, 4-6; L.7.1-5

ADDITIONAL INFORMATION

Concept Map of Thrown to the Wind: Part 4: A New World

Can Etienne save his sister in time? What will his and his family's lives be like in this new and strange land.

KEY LEARNING(S)	UNIT ESSENTIAL QUESTIONS	OPTIONAL INSTRUCTION TOOLS
WRAP-UP PROJECT The teacher or the students will choose a wrap-up project from the list provided.		
LEARNING OBJECTIVES Students will connect the themes in the novel and/or identify crucial scenes, characters, settings, etc. and explain their significance.		
PROJECT IDEAS • Movie Poster • Movie/Documentary Trailer • Diorama • Persuasive Letter • Interview a Character		
COMMON CORE STANDARDS CCSS.ELA-Literacy.SL.7.1a-d, 4-6; L.7.1-3		

ADDITIONAL INFORMATION

Part 1: The Flight

Objectives:

Interpret visual sources to understand historical context.

Interpret primary and secondary sources.

Compare and contrast primary and secondary sources and analyze the purpose each type of source.

Evaluate the accuracy and usefulness of secondary sources in understanding historical events.

Understand the thought process behind sailors creating constellations.

Create your own constellation and accompanying mythology.

Use narrative techniques to write a captivating story.

Handouts:

- *Thrown to the Wind*, Image 1
- Historical Background for Part 1 with Discussion Questions OR Annotated Historical Background for Part 1 with Discussion Questions
- Discussion Questions by chapter
- Copy of *The Log of a Cabin Boy*, by Elford Eddy, 1929, first 9 pages – pdf is available for free download at Google Books https://books.google.com/books/about/The_Log_of_a_Cabin_Boy.html?id=Jug7AQAAMAAJ
- Discussion Questions for *The Log of a Cabin Boy*
- Comparative Essay Prompt
- "Constellation Project Instructions" with Orion Image, Star Chart, and Star Chart without Constellations.
    - A Start Chart is available for free download by *reestarcharts.com* at: https://freestarcharts.com/messier-42
    - Or at "Cloudy Nights," *Astronomics*: https://www.cloudynights.com/articles/cat/articles/observing-skills/free-mag-7-star-charts-r1021

Day 1

1. **Bell Ringer:** Students will examine the image in the handout "*Thrown to the Wind,* Image 1" and answer the questions. Follow up with a discussion of students' answers.
2. Handout to each student a copy of the **"Historical Background for Part 1"** or the **"Annotated Historical Background for Part 1"** and a copy of the **"Discussion Questions"** and tell students that as they read, they should note any unfamiliar or important words.
    a. <u>With Annotation Guide</u> – Use the annotation guide to identify unknown or important words.
    b. <u>Without Annotation Guide</u> - Underline all the words that appear to be technical history terms (<u>Scaffolded</u>: Use the highlighted words). Use the context around the word to create a guess definition then look up the word in the dictionary.
3. Students should answer the discussion questions after they have finished reading. If time is short, students may be asked to complete the questions for homework.
4. Conduct a class discussion of the questions.

Days 2 - 8

1. As students read each section (one or more chapters) ask them to answer the corresponding **"Discussion Questions."** Students could read the chapters at home or in class. The discussion questions may be given out after the students have completed the reading or ahead of time.
2. Conduct a full class discussion or small group round table discussions of the questions.

Day 9

1. Have students read the first 9 pages of *The Log of a Cabin Boy* and answer the discussion questions provided in this resource.
2. Conduct a class discussion of student responses.

3. Use the **"Comparison Essay Prompt"** as a summative assessment.

Optional Constellation Project
1. Have students take a look at the image of Orion and the corresponding star chart provided. Tell students to look at the start chart and see how the stars have been connected to form the shape of the hunter. Then tell them to look at the image of Orion and notice how the image has been drawn over the stars.

2. Hand out the print-out of the inverted star map. Tell students that each of the black dots represent stars. Then tell students to look at the stars and try to create a unique image using lines to connect the dots.

3. Tell students to describe the image they drew and what it is supposed to represent.

4. Finally, have students create a short mythology story about the image.

. . He admired pirates . . They sailed the high seas and the low seas, saw the world, had a heap of fun, wore rings in their noses, drank rum, sang about fifteen dead men. . . .

Image from *The Log of a Cabin Boy*

Name _____ Class _____ Date _____

Thrown to the Wind, Image 1

La Rochelle, The Harbour Entrance, by Jean Baptist Camille Corot
The Yorck Project (2002)

Answer the following questions:

1. What purposes do the towers serve in this image? Why do you think this city would build towers like these on either side of the mouth to the inner harbor?

2. What else can you learn about this city, based on the visual elements present in the image?

3. Would you want to live in this city? Why or why not?

Name: _____

Class: _____

Date: _____

Teacher's Section!!

Completeness _____

Comprehension _____

Clarity/Legibility _____

Total Score: _____

Annotation Notes

Annotation Key:
<u>Underline</u> – key words, phrases, sentences, or dates that are important to understanding the passage. Explain in your own words why this is important in the *Annotation Notes*.
[Brackets] – Important ideas or passages. Explain its importance in the *Annotation Notes*.
Numbers[1] – to mark the chronological sequence of events or ideas
Asterisks* - use to mark the top 1-3 most important statements. Explain its significance in the *Annotation Notes*.
??? – sections or ideas you don't understand. Write out your questions in the *Annotation Notes*.
Checkmark – answers to the discussion questions listed at the end of the article or questions you might have asked while reading. In your own words write out the answer to your question in the *Annotation Notes*.
(Circle) – Words you don't understand. First use the context to guess the meaning, then use a dictionary to look up the word. Write both out in the *Annotation Notes* section.
!!! – Surprising, new, or interesting ideas

Historical Background for

Thrown to the Wind Part 1:
History of Religious Persecution in France

1 **History of the Religious Wars in**
2 **France/Europe**

3 Throughout history, differing religions have come to
4 conflict (sometimes philosophically and sometimes
5 physically). In some cases, conflict will even arise within
6 one religion: a conflict so great it might divide that
7 religion into different "sects." Why do these conflicts
8 arise? In the case of the European Wars of Religion, the
9 conflict arose in large part because of one man (and the
10 men that inspired his doctrines), Martin Luther. Not to be
11 confused with Martin Luther King Jr., the great African
12 American reformer and social activist for civil rights,
13 Martin Luther was born in Germany in 1483. When
14 Luther was 24-years-old, he was ordained as a Roman
15 Catholic priest. For a long time before this, Roman
16 Catholicism was the dominant religion in Europe.
17 Catholic monarchs ruled the majority of countries in
18 Europe.

19   After more than a decade in the priesthood, Martin
20 Luther came to reject many of the Catholic teachings. In
21 particular, Luther rejected the Catholic practice of selling
22 indulgences, "a way to reduce the amount of punishment
23 one has to undergo for sins" in the afterlife.[1] The Catholics
24 believed that if someone dies without being purified, then
25 their soul would be sent to a place called Purgatory. There,
26 their soul would be purified, and any sins they committed
27 before dying would be punished before their soul could go
28 to Heaven. These indulgences started as a way to reward
29 Catholics who did good deeds. However, many Catholic
30 rulers would sell them in order to fund their government
31 projects.[2]

First Impressions
Central Ideas (CI) / Topic
What is the CI/Topic?

_____
_____
_____

Textual Evidence (Use the page and line #s as a reference)

_____
_____
_____
_____

Purpose (POV)
**Circle ONE
  A. Entertain
  B. Persuade
  C. Inform

Textual Evidence (Use the page and line #s as a reference)

_____
_____
_____
_____

---

[1] Edward Peters, *A Modern Guide to Indulgences: Rediscovering this Often Misinterpreted Teaching*, (Chicago: Hillenbrand Books, 2008), 13.
[2] Fr. Enrico dal Covolo, S.D.B, The Historical Origin of Indulgences, (Catholic Culture, 2019).

Name: _____

Annotation Notes		Reading Notes
	32 In 1516, a Dominican friar was sent to Germany to	I Wonder
	33 sell indulgences to help rebuild St. Peter's Basilica in	
	34 Rome. The Archbishop of Mainz was deeply in debt due	
	35 to the project and had requested help from the Church.[3]	
	36 As a form of protest, Martin Luther wrote what is now	
	37 called the **Ninety-Five Theses**, where he debated several	
	38 Catholic doctrines (including the practice of indulgences).	
	39 He also discussed the theology of grace through faith: the	
	40 idea that people did not need indulgences or a priest to	
	41 intercede on their behalf. He believed that all people	
	42 needed to go to Heaven was faith in God and that all	
	43 Christians should have the right and ability to read the	
	44 Bible in their own language. This document spread	
	45 throughout Europe and led other scholars to debate and	
	46 discuss these issues. The Catholic Church eventually	
	47 rejected Luther's doctrines in the **Edict of Worms** issued	
	48 in May 1521 but not before he accrued many followers,	
	49 including German Prince Frederick III. This ex-	
	50 communication led to the Catholic-Protestant Schism by	I Notice
	51 condemning anyone who subscribed to Luther's	
	52 doctrines. This was called the Protestant Reformation.	
	53 Many different sects of Protestantism formed during	
	54 this time of conflict, including Calvinism. Inspired by	
	55 Martin Luther, John Calvin added to Luther's theology of	
	56 grace through faith by outlining the doctrine of	
	57 predestination. The theory of predestination states that God	
	58 "elected" or chose who would receive salvation in the	
	59 afterlife even before the world was formed.[4] The followers	
	60 of John Calvin were called Protestant Calvinists, though	
	61 they were also called Reformists or (in France) **Huguenots**.	
	62 Guillaume Farel, from the French Alps, was the first	
	63 reformer to go to Geneva in 1532, and, so, the Religious	
	64 Wars spread to France.[5]	
	65 From 1562 through 1598, violence, famine, and disease	
	66 killed an estimated three million people, making the French	
	67 Religious Wars the deadliest of the Reformation period.	
	68 Politics between powerful noble families, in the struggle	
	69 for the succession to the throne, also added to this conflict.	
	70 The wealthy, ambitious, and fervently Roman Catholic	
	71 House of Guise went up against the less wealthy House of	
	72 Condé, while the moderates tried to prevent bloodshed. The	
	73 conflict ended when Henry of Navarre of the House of	
	74 Condé was crowned King **Henry IV** of France. Upon	
	75 taking the throne, he converted to Catholicism and issued	

lopaedia Britannica, 2007).
n's Theology: Predestination." *Place for Truth.* (September 20, 2017).
e Stature," The Huguenot Fellowship. (nd).

Name: _____

Annotation Notes		Reading Notes
	76 the **Edict of Nantes**, which provided provisions to protect
77 the rights of Protestants in France.

78 **The Siege of La Rochelle**

79   The city of La Rochelle, situated on the Atlantic coast,
80 was a wealthy trade city, and the second or third largest city
81 in France, with over 30,000 inhabitants. It was also a
82 Huguenot stronghold. While most nobility remained
83 Roman Catholics, the growing merchant and trade guild
84 families in La Rochelle were mostly Protestant.

85   The assassination of Henry IV in 1610 and advent (rise)
86 of King Louis XIII under the regency of his Catholic
87 mother, Marie de' Medici, brought about the return of
88 intense persecution. Louis XIII and his Chief Minister,
89 Cardinal Richelieu, wanted to suppress the Huguenots.[6]

90   In 1627 the King's forces surrounded the city, building
91 entrenchments 7 miles long, fortified with 11 forts and 18
92 redoubts, and stationing 7,000 soldiers with 600 horses and
93 24 cannons. As hostilities broke out, a sea wall was erected,
94 cutting the city off from receiving food and essential
95 supplies. The King increased the army guarding the city to
96 30,000 men. The siege lasted 14 months, during which
97 22,000 people died due to casualties, famine, and disease.
98 Only 5000 people survived the siege of La Rochelle.[7]

99   At the end of the siege, the King ordered the walls of
100 the city be broken down, and he removed all the
101 Huguenots' privileges except the freedom of worship.
102 Cardinal Richelieu's power and influence increased
103 significantly as a result of the siege.[8]

104 **Rise of King Louis XIV**

105   Louis XIV inherited the throne from his father, Louis
106 XIII, in 1643, when he was only four years old. His mother,
107 Anne, was a Spanish princess of the Habsburg family.
108 During her regency, she relied heavily on the advice of her
109 Chief Minister, Cardinal Mazarin, who was the protégé of
110 Cardinal Richelieu. In 1651, Louis XIV officially came of
111 age as the King, but, as he was only 13, he was still heavily
112 controlled by his mother. In 1660, Louis married Maria
113 Theresa, daughter of Spanish King Philip IV. Cardinal | I Wonder

I Notice |

---

[6] "The Siege of La Rochelle," The Huguenot Fellowship. (April 24, 2018).
[7] "The Siege of La Rochelle," The Huguenot Fellowship. (April 24, 2018).
[8] Macgregor, Mary. "The Siege of La Rochelle," *The Story of France*, by Mary Macgregor. *The Baldwin Project* (New York: Frederick A. Stokes Company, 1911).

Name: _____

Annotation Notes		Closing Impressions

114 Mazarin died in 1661, and it was at this point that Louis
115 XIV started to take control of France in his own right.

116   France was in political disarray and economically
117 bankrupt. Louis XIV announced that he would rule without
118 a chief minister and began to institute administrative and
119 fiscal reforms. He would remove the Superintendent of
120 Finances, Nicolas Fouquet, charging him with
121 embezzlement. Later, he would create the lesser title of
122 Controller-General of Finances and appoint Jean-Baptiste
123 Colbert to the position. New and more efficient taxes were
124 instituted to begin reducing France's debt.

125   As part of his plan to unify and strengthen his kingdom,
126 Louis XIV also instituted his anti-Reformation policy. As
127 early as 1655, Protestant churches built outside the places
128 specified in the Edict of Nantes were torn down, and access
129 to religious services was restricted.[9] Many Protestant
130 Huguenots had to conduct their services and the education
131 of their children in secret. Then upon taking full control of
132 France, Louis XIV began issuing decrees and royal claims
133 to forbid Protestant religious worship and attendance at
134 services. He also removed dignity and freedom of
135 conscience, a legal right granted to Huguenots in the Edit
136 of Nantes (1598).[10] Calvinist reformist leaders were
137 arrested, and many Huguenots began fleeing France for the
138 Netherlands and England.

139   Conditions for Huguenots continued to decline as more
140 members of the Reformed Church were arrested and
141 executed. Huguenots fought back, leading to uprisings that
142 were put down, and rebels rounded up and burned at the
143 stake. Then the Huguenots were forced to provide lodgings
144 to the King's soldiers, called Dragoons. In 1685, the King
145 revoked the Edict of Nantes with the signing of the **Edict**
146 **of Fontainebleau.**[11]

Closing Impressions

Central Ideas (CI) / Topic
Has your understanding of the CI/Topic Changed? If so, how? If not, provide an additional piece of textual evidence on the lines below to support your previous CI.

_____
_____
_____

Textual Evidence to support your CI (Use the page and line #s as a reference)

_____
_____
_____

Author Bias
Does the author show bias toward any of the people groups mentioned?

_____
_____
_____

Textual Evidence (Use the page and line #s as a reference)

_____
_____

Briefly Summarize the Passage (Use the back or a separate sheet of paper for more space)

---

[9] "The Edict of Nantes (1598)," *The 16th Century*. Museeprotestant, (France: n.d. Accessed 10/27/2018).
[10] "The period of the Revocation of the Edict of Nantes (1661-1700)," *The 17th Century*. (Museeprotestant, France: n.d. Accessed 10/27/2018).
[11] Ibid.

Name _____ Class _____ Date _____

Historical Background for
Thrown to the Wind Part 1:
The Flight

History of the Religious Wars in France/Europe

Throughout history, differing religions have come to conflict (sometimes philosophically and sometimes physically). In some cases, conflict will even arise within one religion: a conflict so great it might divide that religion into different "sects." Why do these conflicts arise? In the case of the European Wars of Religion, the conflict arose in large part because of one man (and the men that inspired his doctrines), Martin Luther. Not to be confused with Martin Luther King Jr., the great African American reformer and social activist for civil rights, Martin Luther was born in Germany in 1483. When Luther was 24 years old, he was ordained as a Roman Catholic priest. For a long time before this, Roman Catholicism was the dominant religion in Europe. Catholic monarchs ruled the majority of countries in Europe.

After more than a decade in the priesthood, Martin Luther came to reject many of the Catholic teachings. In particular, Luther rejected the Catholic practice of selling indulgences, "a way to reduce the amount of punishment one has to undergo for sins" in the afterlife.[1] The Catholics believed that if someone dies without being purified, then their soul would be sent to a place called Purgatory. There, their soul would be purified, and any sins they committed before dying would be punished before their soul could go to Heaven. These indulgences started as a way to reward Catholics who did good deeds. However, many Catholic rulers would sell them in order to fund their government projects.[2]

In 1516, a Dominican friar was sent to Germany to sell indulgences to help rebuild St. Peter's Basilica in Rome. The Archbishop of Mainz was deeply in debt due to the project and had requested help from the Church.[3] As a form of protest, Martin Luther wrote what is now called the **Ninety-Five Theses**, where he debated several Catholic doctrines (including the practice of indulgences). He also discussed the theology of grace through faith: the idea that people did not need indulgences or a priest to intercede on their behalf. He believed that all people needed to go to Heaven was faith in God and that all Christians should have the right and ability to read the Bible in their own language. This document spread throughout Europe and led other scholars to debate and discuss these issues. The Catholic Church eventually rejected Luther's doctrines in the **Edict of Worms** issued in May 1521 but not before he accrued many followers, including German Prince Frederick III. This ex-communication led to the Catholic-Protestant Schism by condemning anyone who subscribed to Luther's doctrines. This was called the Protestant Reformation.

Many different sects of Protestantism formed during this time of conflict, including Calvinism. Inspired by Martin Luther, John Calvin added to Luther's theology of grace through faith by outlining the doctrine of predestination. The theory of predestination states that God "elected" or chose who would receive salvation in the afterlife even before the world was formed.[4] The followers of John Calvin were called Protestant Calvinists, though they were also called Reformists or (in France) **Huguenots**. Guillaume Farel, from the French Alps, was the first reformer to go to Geneva in 1532, and, so, the Religious Wars spread to France.[5]

From 1562 through 1598, violence, famine, and disease killed an estimated three million people, making the French Religious Wars the deadliest of the Reformation period. Politics between powerful

---

[1] Edward Peters, *A Modern Guide to Indulgences: Rediscovering this Often Misinterpreted Teaching*, (Chicago: Hillenbrand Books, 2008), 13.
[2] Fr. Enrico dal Covolo, S.D.B, The Historical Origin of Indulgences, (Catholic Culture, 2019).
[3] *Johann Tetzel*, (Encylopaedia Britannica, 2007).
[4] Bertolet, Tim. "Calvin's Theology: Predestination." *Place for Truth.* (September 20, 2017).
[5] "The Reformers on the Stature," The Huguenot Fellowship. (nd).

noble families, in the struggle for the succession to the throne, also added to this conflict. The wealthy, ambitious, and fervently Roman Catholic House of Guise went up against the less wealthy House of Condé, while the moderates tried to prevent bloodshed. The conflict ended when Henry of Navarre of the House of Condé was crowned King **Henry IV** of France. Upon taking the throne, he converted to Catholicism and issued the **Edict of Nantes**, which provided provisions to protect the rights of Protestants in France.

The Siege of La Rochelle

The city of La Rochelle, situated on the Atlantic coast, was a wealthy trade city, and the second or third largest city in France, with over 30,000 inhabitants. It was also a Huguenot stronghold. While most nobility remained Roman Catholics, the growing merchant and trade guild families in La Rochelle were mostly Protestant.

The assassination of Henry IV in 1610 and advent (rise) of King Louis XIII under the regency of his Catholic mother, Marie de' Medici, brought about the return of intense persecution. Louis XIII and his Chief Minister, Cardinal Richelieu, wanted to suppress the Huguenots.[6]

In 1627 the King's forces surrounded the city, building entrenchments 7 miles long, fortified with 11 forts and 18 redoubts, and stationing 7,000 soldiers with 600 horses and 24 cannons. As hostilities broke out, a sea wall was erected, cutting the city off from receiving food and essential supplies. The King increased the army guarding the city to 30,000 men. The siege lasted 14 months, during which 22,000 people died due to casualties, famine, and disease. Only 5000 people survived the siege of La Rochelle.[7]

At the end of the siege, the King ordered the walls of the city be broken down, and he removed all the Huguenots' privileges except the freedom of worship. Cardinal Richelieu's power and influence increased significantly as a result of the siege.[8]

Rise of King Louis XIV

Louis XIV inherited the throne from his father, Louis XIII, in 1643, when he was only four years old. His mother, Anne, was a Spanish princess of the Habsburg family. During her regency, she relied heavily on the advice of her Chief Minister, Cardinal Mazarin, who was the protégé of Cardinal Richelieu. In 1651, Louis XIV officially came of age as the King, but, as he was only 13, he was still heavily controlled by his mother. In 1660, Louis married Maria Theresa, daughter of Spanish King Philip IV. Cardinal Mazarin died in 1661, and it was at this point that Louis XIV started to take control of France in his own right.

France was in political disarray and economically bankrupt. Louis XIV announced that he would rule without a chief minister and began to institute administrative and fiscal reforms. He would remove the Superintendent of Finances, Nicolas Fouquet, charging him with embezzlement. Later, he would create the lesser title of Controller-General of Finances and appoint Jean-Baptiste Colbert to the position. New and more efficient taxes were instituted to begin reducing France's debt.

As part of his plan to unify and strengthen his kingdom, Louis XIV also instituted his anti-Reformation policy. As early as 1655, Protestant churches built outside the places specified in the Edict of Nantes were torn down, and access to religious services was restricted.[9] Many Protestant Huguenots had to conduct their services and the education of their children in secret. Then upon taking full control of France, Louis XIV began issuing decrees and royal claims to forbid Protestant religious worship and attendance at services. He also removed dignity and freedom of conscience, a legal right granted to Huguenots in the Edit of Nantes (1598).[10] Calvinist reformist leaders were

---

[6] "The Siege of La Rochelle," The Huguenot Fellowship. (April 24, 2018).

[7] "The Siege of La Rochelle," The Huguenot Fellowship. (April 24, 2018).

[8] Macgregor, Mary. "The Siege of La Rochelle," *The Story of France*, by Mary Macgregor. *The Baldwin Project*. (New York: Frederick A. Stokes Company, 1911).

[9] "The Edict of Nantes (1598)," *The 16th Century*. Museeprotestant, (France: n.d. Accessed 10/27/2018).

[10] "The period of the Revocation of the Edict of Nantes (1661-1700)," *The 17th Century*. (Museeprotestant, France: n.d. Accessed 10/27/2018).

arrested, and many Huguenots began fleeing France for the Netherlands and England.

Conditions for Huguenots continued to decline as more members of the Reformed Church were arrested and executed. Huguenots fought back, leading to uprisings that were put down, and rebels rounded up and burned at the stake. Then the Huguenots were forced to provide lodgings to the King's soldiers, called Dragoons. In 1685, the King revoked the Edict of Nantes with the signing of the **Edict of Fontainebleau**.[11]

Cardinal Richelieu at the Siege of La Rochelle by Henri-Paul Motte, 1881
Musée d'Orbigny Bernon

---

[11] Ibid.

24

Name _____ Date _____

Discussion Questions

Teacher's Section!!

Completeness _____

Comprehension _____

Clarity/Legibility _____

Total Score: _____

Student Instructions: On the back of this page or a separate sheet of answer the following questions. Be prepared to discuss them with the class. Make sure to put your full name and the date at the top of your answer page.

Vocabulary Assignment: Underline all the words that appear to be technical history terms. (*Scaffolded: Use the highlighted words.*) Whether or not you are already familiar with the word, notice the context around the word to create a guess definition for the word. After that, look up the word in the dictionary and write the exact, relevant definition(s) below your guess.

1. What is the primary purpose of this text (informative, persuasive/argumentative, entertaining)? Does the author(s) reveal his/her bias (opinion) about the Catholics vs. Protestants? If so, what is their bias, and how do you know? If not, how did they maintain a neutral tone? Use textual evidence to support your point.

2. Using the historical summary for part 1, create a timeline of the major events leading up Edict of Fontainebleau.

3. In your own words, describe the top three most significant people, events, or policies that caused the War of Religions. What were the motivations of those involved on both sides? What were the effects or consequences of the wars? Use textual evidence to support your answer.

4. Looking at today, how have the Wars of Religion affected modern society? Do you see any lasting effects today? Explain and support your answer using relevant examples.

5. Did the conflict between Roman Catholics and Protestants unify and/or divide Europe? Explain your answer. Use textual evidence to support your answer.

Name _____

Class _____

Date _____

Teacher's Section!!

Completeness _____

Comprehension _____

Clarity/Legibility _____

Total Score: _____

Discussion Questions Chapter 1

Student Instructions: On the back of this page or a separate sheet of answer the following questions. Be prepared to discuss them with the class. Make sure to put your full name and the date at the top of your answer page.

1. What details does the author use to create a sense of urgency, unease, and/or tension in this opening scene? Cite textual evidence to support your answer.

2. Who is the narrator? Describe the narrator using 3 adjectives. Why did you choose those descriptors? What is the narrator's relationship to Nicolas? Do you think he will keep his promise to Nicolas? Why or why not? Cite textual evidence to support your answer.

3. How does the setting (time and place) of this story relate to the historical summary? Where and when in the series of events listed in the historical summary does this story fit in? In this chapter, Etienne tells a story his grandfather used to tell him about the Siege of La Rochelle. How does Etienne's grandfather's version compare or contrast to the historical account? At the end of the chapter, the Catholic cardinal gives a speech to the town, how does the cardinal's speech foreshadow what is to come? Use textual evidence from both the story and historical summary to support your answer.

4. What French words did you see in the text? Based on context, how would you define those words?

5. Why do you think the author choose the chapter title "Musketeers"? What is the significance of this title? What does it represent or demonstrate?

26

Name _____

Class _____

Date _____

Teacher's Section!!

Completeness _____

Comprehension_____

Clarity/Legibility_____

Total Score: _____

Discussion Questions Chapter 2

Student Instructions: On the back of this page or a separate sheet of answer the following questions. Be prepared to discuss them with the class. Make sure to put your full name and the date at the top of your answer page.

1. What did you learn about the Protestant (Huguenot) vs. Catholic feud from this chapter? What is the Protestant argument against the Catholics? What is the Catholics argument against the Protestants? How does this compare to the historical summary we read at the beginning of the section? Use textual evidence to support your answer.

2. Based on your understanding of the surrounding text (contextual clues), what do you think "maître" means? Why do you think this is an important word? What does it say about Quintal's relationship to Etienne? Support your answer with textual evidence.

3. What is a musketeer? According to the text, why are there so many of them in the city? Why do you think the author had Etienne encounter one? What value does this meeting bring to the story?

www.windyseapublishing.com   *Windy Sea Publishing, LLC*   *Thrown to the Wind Teacher's Resource*

Name _____

Class _____

Date _____

Teacher's Section!!
Completeness _____
Comprehension _____
Clarity/Legibility _____
Total Score: _____

Discussion Questions Chapters 3-4

Student Instructions: On the back of this page or a separate sheet of answer the following questions. Be prepared to discuss them with the class. Make sure to put your full name and the date at the top of your answer page.

1. According to the text, Etienne's Papa calls him "Garcon" which means "boy." It can also mean "waiter" or "male employee or servant." Why might this be considered insulting? Why might Etienne's father use this as a term of endearment? Use textual evidence to support your answer.

2. Why did the author choose to use the story of Daniel and the Lion's Den in this chapter? How does this foreshadow what's to come? What is the significance of this story to their faith and believes? What lesson does Etienne's father take from this story? Do you agree or disagree with him and why?

3. Why doesn't Etienne keep his promise to his cousin Nicolas? What would have happened if he had stayed with Nicolas instead of returning to his family?

28

Name _____

Class _____

Date _____

Teacher's Section!!
Completeness _____
Comprehension _____
Clarity/Legibility _____
Total Score: _____

Discussion Questions Chapters 5-8

Student Instructions: On the back of this page or a separate sheet of answer the following questions. Be prepared to discuss them with the class. Make sure to put your full name and the date at the top of your answer page.

1. In chapter 5, why does Etienne drop the stone he picked up at Nicolas' house? What does the stone symbolize? Use textual evidence to support your answer.

2. In chapter 6, Etienne has a second chance to go to Nicolas. Why does he give it up this time? What would his life have been like if he had jumped off and swam back?

3. In chapter 8, why did Petry, the officer who went below deck, not report the Huguenots? Use textual evidence to support your answer.

4. At the end of chapter 8, Etienne asks his father "why the Catholics care what we practice?" How would you answer that question if you were talking to Etienne? Throughout the book we have often heard the Catholics accuse the Huguenots of practicing "heresy." How might that help answer this question? In his answer, Etienne's father accuses the Catholic Pope of Blaspheming. Is there a difference in the Catholic accusations versus the Protestants' accusations? If so, what is the difference? If not, what does that say about this conflict between Protestants and Catholics? Use textual evidence from the story and from your historical summary of part 1 to support your answer.

5. After reading the first eight chapters of this book, would you call Etienne an active or a passive character? Does he cause or try to cause change to happen in his life or is he caught up in his circumstances? Use textual evidence to support your answer.

Name _____

Class _____

Date _____

Teacher's Section!!

Completeness _____

Comprehension _____

Clarity/Legibility _____

Total Score: _____

Discussion Questions Chapter 9

Student Instructions: On the back of this page or a separate sheet of answer the following questions. Be prepared to discuss them with the class. Make sure to put your full name and the date at the top of your answer page.

1. Back in the 17th century in Europe, young boys were expected to train in and, eventually, take over their fathers' profession. Imagine that your only option for a career is your parent's job. What would that look like? How does it make you feel? How might it make your best friend feel or your sister or brother? How might this social expectation affect Etienne? How does this affect Etienne's actions? How does it affect his relationships with the other Huguenot children? Use textual evidence from the section one historical summary and from the story to support your answer.

2. Etienne believes that his brother's death is his fault. Do you agree or disagree with him? Why or why not? Does this change your opinion of Etienne? Why or why not? Use textual details to support your answer.

3. Why did the author choose to use a flashback in this chapter? What value does this flashback bring to the plot and/or character development of Etienne? Support your answer with textual evidence.

30

Name _____

Class _____

Date _____

Teacher's Section!!

Completeness _____

Comprehension _____

Clarity/Legibility _____

Total Score: _____

Discussion Questions Chapter 10

Student Instructions: On the back of this page or a separate sheet of answer the following questions. Be prepared to discuss them with the class. Make sure to put your full name and the date at the top of your answer page.

1. When Etienne was confronted by the captain, why did he not reveal the names of the boys who locked him up in the crate? Would you have told? What are the possible consequences of NOT speaking up against Francois?

2. What motivated Etienne to ask to be a cabin boy? What would you have done in this situation? Do you think this makes Etienne an active or passive character? Why or why not? Use textual evidence to support your answer.

3. On page 50, Captain Carteret lists the duties of a cabin boy. Do you think Etienne would make a good fit as a cabin boy? Why or why not? Use textual evidence to support your answer.

Name _____

Class _____

Date _____

Teacher's Section!!

Completeness _____

Comprehension _____

Clarity/Legibility _____

Discussion Questions Chapter 11

Total Score: _____

Student Instructions: On the back of this page or a separate sheet of answer the following questions. Be prepared to discuss them with the class. Make sure to put your full name and the date at the top of your answer page.

1. Captain Carteret teaches Etienne how to track a path using a map, a compass, and, in the next chapter, geometry. Why does he say that tracking a path is so important? How might these skills help Etienne out later in life both literally and metaphorically?

2. On page 54, The Captain teaches Etienne to tie a bow-line knot. What does he tell Etienne this knot is useful for? What might this lesson foreshadow about what might happen to Etienne later in the story?

3. On pages 54-55, Etienne learns the ship names for things. Use a dictionary to look up all possible definitions for these words, choose two (not including "head" or "foot"), and attempt to come up with a reason why sailors might have called these ship elements by those names.

4. Why do you think people back in history connected the stars together to form constellations? And why would they attach stories to the constellations to stories? What might this have helped them do? Defend your argument.

5. At the end of the chapter, Captain Carteret talks to Etienne about his nephew. Do you think the nephew's death was the Captain's fault? Why or why not? How does this story relate to Etienne? What lessons does Etienne learn or start to learn from the Captain's story? What does this story cause him to reveal to the Captain? Use textual evidence to support your answer.

Thrown to the Wind Teacher's Resource   *Windy Sea Publishing, LLC*   www.windyseapublishing.com

Name _____

Class _____

Date _____

Teacher's Section!!

Completeness _____

Comprehension _____

Clarity/Legibility _____

Total Score: _____

Discussion Questions Chapters 12-13

Student Instructions: On the back of this page or a separate sheet of answer the following questions. Be prepared to discuss them with the class. Make sure to put your full name and the date at the top of your answer page.

1. In chapter 12 on pg. 65, Captain Carteret distinguishes adulthood from childhood by defining it as having integrity, or "standing by [one's] word." Do you agree or disagree with this statement? Why or why not? Do you think the Captain's chastisement is fair or unfair to Etienne? Explain why or why not using textual evidence to support your answer.

2. Why do you think Etienne's father would not make eye contact with Captain Carteret? Why was he so hesitant to respond to the Captain's offer?

3. Was it fair or unfair of Etienne's father to reject to Captain Carteret's offer to Etienne? What effect might this refusal have on the story and Etienne and his father's relationship? Explain your position using textual evidence to support your answer.

Name _____

Class _____

Date _____

Teacher's Section!! 33

Completeness _____

Comprehension _____

Clarity/Legibility _____

Total Score: _____

Discussion Questions "The Log of a Cabin Boy"

Student Instructions: On the back of this page or a separate sheet of answer the following questions. Be prepared to discuss them with the class. Make sure to put your full name and the date at the top of your answer page.

1. This story was published in 1922 the same year construction on The Schmidt Lithography Co. clock tower began. Max Schmidt started out as a cabin boy and eventually went on to create the very successful lithography company. With that knowledge, and after reading the brief introduction to the story on pages 1 and 2, why do you suppose this story was written? What is the bias and purpose of this short biographical narrative? Use textual evidence to support your answer.

2. What value do the pictures/sketches in this narrative bring to the story? Why might the author have decided to include them? How might they help serve the story's purpose? What story do they tell?

3. What duties were cabin boys expected to accomplish while on the ship according to this story? Does it sound like an easy job? In the story Max Schmidt made $10 a month which means that in a year he would have earned just $120 when the average wage of the time was a little over $3,000 a year. Do you think he was making a fair income for the tasks he was completing? Do you think he made the right decision staying in America? Explain your position.

Thrown to the Wind Teacher's Resource   Windy Sea Publishing, LLC   www.windyseapublishing.com

34

Name _____

Class _____

Date _____

Teacher's Section!!

Topic: _____

Evidence: _____

Organization: _____

Language: _____

Total Score: _____

Essay Prompt

Compare and Contrast: Etienne and Max Schmidt

Student Instructions: Write an essay answering the following prompt. Be prepared to discuss it with the class. Make sure to put your full name and the date at the top of your answer page.

After reading part 1 of *Thrown to the Wind* and the first 9 pages of *The Log of a Cabin Boy*, compare and contrast Etienne's story so far with that of Max Schmidt. How are their stories similar? How are they different? Based on the similarities and differences, make a prediction about what you think will happen in Etienne's story. Use textual evidence from both sources to support your answer.

Name _____

Class _____

Date _____

Teacher's Section!!

Preparation & Collaboration: _____

Content & Completion: _____

Presentation & Articulation: _____

Total Score: _____

Constellation Project

Student Instructions: As individuals or in groups, follow the instructions below to create your own constellation and accompanying myth.

1. Look at the image of Orion and the corresponding star chart provided. Examine how the stars have been connected to form the shape of the hunter. Notice how the image has been drawn over the stars.

2. On the print-out of the inverted star map, each of the black dots represent stars. Look at the stars and try to create a unique image using lines to connect the dots.

3. Describe the image and what it is supposed to represent.

4. Create a short mythology story about the image.

    a. Who is the hero?

    b. Who is the subject of the constellation? It is not always the hero that gets put into the star, sometimes it is the antagonist that is memorialized. In the case of Orion, it was his nemesis Scorpio that was put into the stars first.

    c. What happened? Write a short story describing your mythology.

    d. What was significant about this story and why did this character from the story get put into the stars?

Thrown to the Wind Teacher's Resource   *Windy Sea Publishing, LLC*   www.windyseapublishing.com

Image of Orion

An Engraving of Orion from Johann Bayer's *Uranometria*, 1603.
US Navel Observatory Library

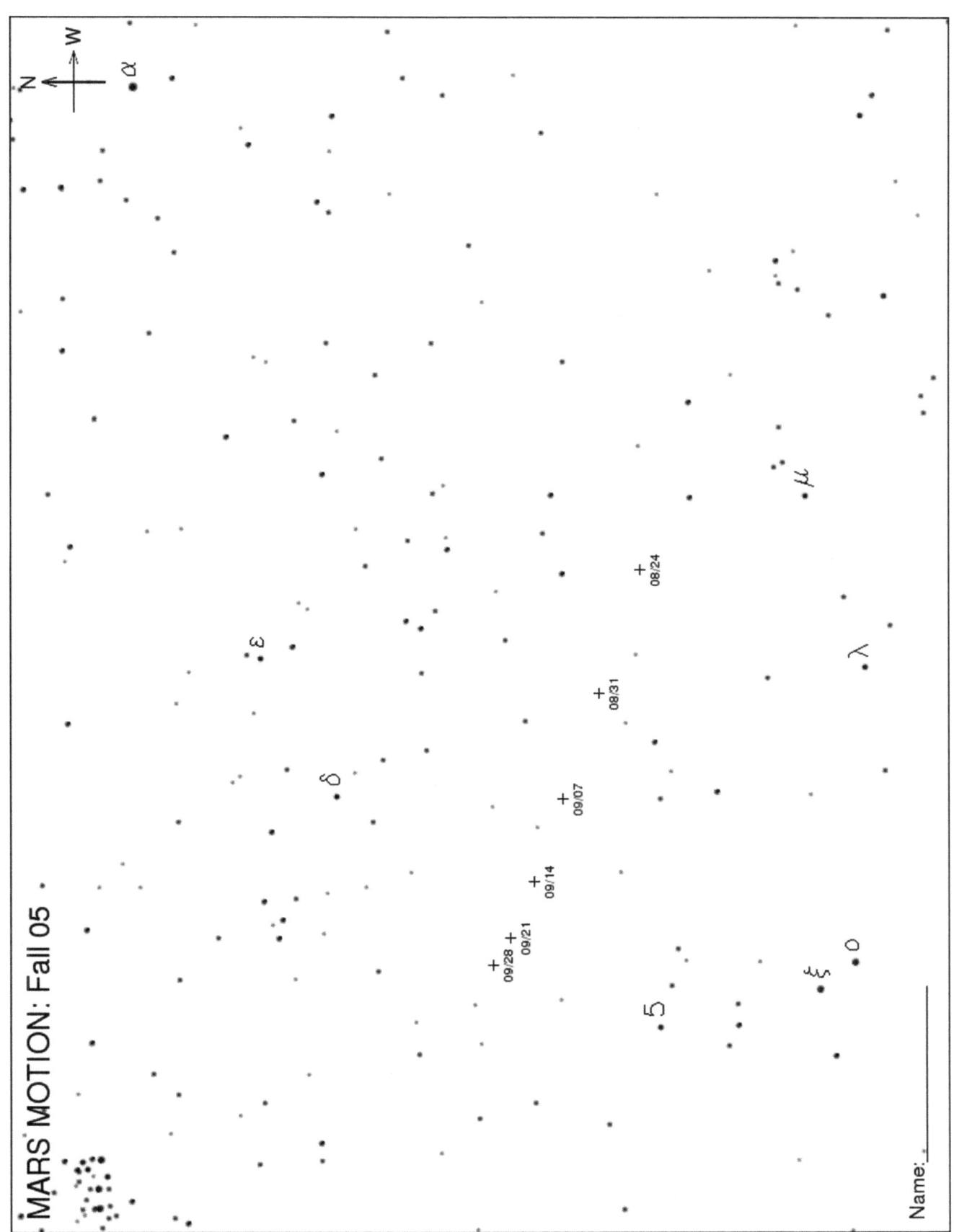

Part 2: Refugees

Objectives:

Interpret visual sources to understand historical context.

Interpret primary and secondary sources.

Compare and contrast primary and secondary sources and analyze the purpose each type of source.

Evaluate the accuracy and usefulness of secondary sources in understanding historical events.

Handouts:
- *Thrown to the Wind*, Image 2
- Historical Background for Part 2 with Discussion Questions OR Annotated Historical Background for Part 2 with Discussion Questions
- Research Project
- Argumentative Essay Prompt
- Discussion Questions by chapter
- Research Project
- Argumentative Essay

Day 1

1. **Bell Ringer:** Students will examine the image in the handout *"Thrown to the Wind, Image 2"* and answer the questions. Follow up with a discussion of students' answers.

2. Handout to each student a copy of the **"Historical Background for Part 2"** or the **"Annotated Historical Background for Part 2"** and tell students that as they read, they should note any unfamiliar or important words.

    a. <u>With Annotation Guide</u> – Use the annotation guide to identify unknown or important words.

    b. <u>Without Annotation Guide</u> - Underline all the words that appear to be technical history terms (<u>Scaffolded</u>: Use the highlighted words). Use the context around the word to create a guess definition then look up the word in the dictionary.

3. Introduce the **Compare and Contrast France and the Netherlands Research Project** and break students into small groups.

4. Student Groups will research their topics and complete their portion of the comparison chart.

Day 2

1. Divide up the groups so that each new group contains at least one person from Day 1.

2. Students then will share the information they researched on day one and will complete the comparison chart with the information provided from the remaining group members. For scaffolded or differentiated learning, the teacher may develop new groups that are centered on only one topic (this will then become a three-day activity).

3. Answer the questions for each of the following the topics, comparing and contrasting the different cultures.

Optional Day 3

1. Change up topic groups bringing one representative/scholar/expert from each topic and making new groups with one representative from each previous group.

2. Students teach their new group about their topic and share their answers.

3. Class discussion:

    a. First: groups decide upon a representative (scaffolded) or teacher chooses a representative (if trying to assess full student comprehension – can add to groups that everyone should know the answer to all the questions and top students should make sure lower students know it all).

    b. Next: The teacher asks random questions from the list to each group representative to check for comprehension and ensure all students hear all answers.

Day 4
1. Character Analysis Essay Prompt

Days 5 - 9
1. As students read each section (one or more chapters) ask them to answer the corresponding **"Discussion Questions."** Students could read the chapters at home or in class. The discussion questions may be given out after the students had completed the reading or ahead of time.
2. Conduct a full class discussion or small group round table discussions of the questions.

Day 10
1. Essay/Story Rewrite.
2. Conduct a class discussion of student responses.

Optional Trade Game/Simulation
1. Persuasive Letter: Students will write a persuasive letter to a wealthy merchant to convince them to patronize their voyage.
    a. Students should focus on the benefits of their journey and explain the precautions they will take to mitigate any potential problems or dangers.
    b. Students should be sure to emphasize the benefit this journey will bring to the patron.
2. Adventure Journal: Students will write a short story (in the form of personal journal entries) about their character's adventures in the New World.
    a. Students will imagine that this is their first time in a new land that is geographically very different than what they have seen before.
    b. They will then write an adventure journal describing this new land and their character's adventure in it.
    c. Remind students to use a lot of sensory details and imagery in order to capture the setting. Make sure the emphasize that they include ALL FIVE senses in their description.
3. Trade Game/Simulation is printed as a separate supplemental resource.
    a. Instructor manual
    b. Story guide
    c. Stat sheets
    d. Cards
    e. Reprint of optional persuasive letter assignment
    f. Reprint of optional adventure journal.

Name _____ Class _____ Date _____

Thrown to the Wind, Image 2

Texel Harbor, Netherlands, 17th Century
Return to Amsterdam of the Second Expedition to the East Indies (1599),
by Hendrick Cornelisz Vroom
Rijksmuseum, Amsterdam

Answer the following questions:

1. How many different types of ships are there in this image? Describe the characteristics of the different types of ships.

2. Based on your answer above, what can you infer about Texel Harbor? For example, in what ways do people make their living? How successful are they?

3. What is the point of view portrayed in the image? For example, does the artist have a favorable or negative view of the activity in the harbor? What evidence or visual features support your conclusion?

Name: _____

Class: _____

Date: _____

Teacher's Section!!

Completeness _____

Comprehension _____

Clarity/Legibility _____

Total Score: _____

Annotation Notes

Annotation Key:
Underline – key words, phrases, sentences, or dates that are important to understanding the passage. Explain in your own words why this is important in the *Annotation Notes*.
[Brackets] – Important ideas or passages. Explain its importance in the *Annotation Notes*.
Numbers[1] – to mark the chronological sequence of events or ideas
Asterisks* - use to mark the top 1-3 most important statements. Explain its significance in the *Annotation Notes*.
??? – sections or ideas you don't understand. Write out your questions in the *Annotation Notes*.
Checkmark – answers to the discussion questions listed at the end of the article or questions you might have asked while reading. In your own words write out the answer to your question in the *Annotation Notes*.
Circle – Words you don't understand. First use the context to guess the meaning, then use a dictionary to look up the word. Write both out in the *Annotation Notes* section.
!!! – Surprising, new, or interesting ideas

Historical Background for
Thrown to the Wind Part 2:
France: Society, Government, and Economics

1   **Social Class**

2   *Structure/Overview*

3   French social class structure in the 17th century was
4   rigid and complicated. There was little to no social mobility
5   between the four primary classes: The Catholic clergy
6   (cardinals and bishops), the aristocracy (the nobility), the
7   *bourgeoisie* (the middle class), and the *prolétariat* (the
8   lower class).

9   *Titles*

10 The nobility were the only people honored with titles.
11 Whereas today we might address someone as sir, ma'am,
12 mister (Mr.), misses (Mrs.), or miss (Ms.) these used to be
13 titles reserved for English nobility only. Likewise, France
14 had similar titles for their nobility. These titles were passed
15 down from father to son when the father passed away. In a
16 few French regions that had previously been independent
17 before France conquered them, there were a few titles
18 passed down the female line, but this was rare.

19 The king and his family had even more complicated
20 titles. Formally, he would be presented to the room as "The
21 King His Most Christian Majesty." If addressed directly by
22 another royal the first time, they would call him "The King
23 Your Most Christian Majesty." Every time after the first
24 introduction, he could be called "Your/His Majesty," "Sire,"
25 or "Monsieur le Roi." Whereas the king and queen were
26 addressed with the title "Your Majesty," the princes and
27 princesses would be addressed as "Your Highness."[1]

28 Other French nobility would be addressed as
29 Monsieur, Madame, or Mademoiselle, unless the king's
30 brother and wife were present. More formally, they would

First Impressions
Central Ideas (CI) / Topic
What is the CI/Topic?

_____
_____
_____
_____

Textual Evidence (Use the page and line #s as a reference)

_____
_____
_____
_____
_____

Purpose (POV)
**Circle ONE
o   Entertain
o   Persuade
o   Inform

Textual Evidence (Use the page and line #s as a reference)

_____
_____
_____
_____
_____

---

[1] "The Art of Addressing French Nobility," *Party Like 1660.*

| Annotation Notes | | Reading Notes |

31 be called by their first name, followed by "de" and the
32 name of their house of property.

33   The *bourgeoisie* and *prolétariat* did not have titles,
34 though teachers were called *maistre*, as a form of respect.
35 Among the Protestants, the title of "Brother" was often
36 used as a form of association. Additionally, the term
37 "Goodwife" was frequently used to refer to a married
38 woman.

I Wonder

39   It is interesting to note that, in France, it was generally
40 impolite to call people by name in their presence. One
41 knew who was being addressed by the use of eye contact.
42 Names were used only when the person was not present or
43 in order to get someone's attention when eye contact was
44 not possible. Additionally, nicknames were seldom used in
45 17th century France.

46   *The Catholic Clergy*

I Notice

47   The Catholic Clergy was at the top of the social
48 structure along with the nobility. They played such an
49 important role in French society that they even dominated a
50 whole branch of the French government called The First
51 Estate (more on this in the government section). Many of
52 these bishops and clergymen "considered themselves
53 socially, intellectually, and morally superior to other
54 members of [the government and] held that the First Estate
55 should maintain its independence and have a broader role
56 in government and society."[2]

57   The Catholic Clergy, much like the government, had a
58 hierarchy or ranking system that puts some people over
59 others as more respected, wealthier, and more powerful.

60   The highest authority in the Church belongs to the
61 Bishop of Rome, the Pope, who "has full, supreme and
62 universal power over the whole church, a power which he
63 can always exercise unhindered."[3]

64   After the Pope, the order goes:[4]

65   • Cardinals
66   • Archbishops
67   • Bishops
68   • Priests

---

[2]. Michael Hayden and Malcolm R. Greenshields, *French Historical Studies*: "The Clergy of Early Seventeenth Century France: Self-Perception and Society's Perception." Vol. 18, No. 1 (Spring, 1993), pp. 145-172

[3] Catechism of the Catholic Church, no.882.

[4] CE Editors, *Explaining the Hierarchy of the Church*. Catholic Exchange. Feb. 17th, 2005.

Annotation Notes			Reading Notes
	69	• Deacons	
	70	• Laity	I Wonder
	71	*The Aristocracy*	
	72	The aristocracy was among the top of society. In	
	73	addition to dominating the Second Estate of the	
	74	government, the aristocracy had many specific legal and	
	75	financial privileges. Among all French citizens, they were	
	76	the only ones allowed to hunt, to wear a sword, and to own	
	77	land or hold certain military, civic, or clerical positions.	
	78	Additionally, they were exempt from the *taille* or tax. They	
	79	could also issue additional taxes on those who lived and	
	80	worked on their land.	
	81	Nobles were required to swear loyalty to the king and	
	82	often had to serve in the military or pay a "blood tax" to	
	83	support the military. Additionally, the king could revoke a	
	84	noble's title if they engaged in specific tasks like manual	
	85	labor.[5]	I Notice

Fun Fact: Silly Court Rules (lines 86–112)

86 **Fun Fact: Silly Court Rules**

87–90   King Louis XIV's (The Sun King) court of nobles in Versailles was full of precise rules or etiquette that determined one's status in court. How well a noble could follow all the rules largely determined their rank and status among the other nobles. Here are some of the weirdest rules.

91–94   1. Knocking with one's knuckles on a door was impolite. Instead, courtiers were expected to lightly scratch on the door frame as a way to announce their presence. As a result, many courtiers grew out one of their nails to use for this purpose.[6]

95–99   2. Every part of the king's daily tasks were on display to nobles, including getting up in the morning, washing up, dressing and undressing, eating, and even using the toilet. The king would grant courtiers with special favor the honor of handing the king his shirt as he dressed or a special place close to him while he sat on the toilet.[7]

100–106   3. Only some people had the right to sit. The King and Queen would sit in a cushioned armchair. Close relatives of the king, such as his brother or sons and daughters, would be allowed to sit in an armless chair. Lastly, duchesses would be allowed to sit on stools. Everyone else would have to stand. Furthermore, a noble had to be invited to sit by a higher ranking official. So, even if one was of rank, they could be denied a seat if they insulted the higher-ranking courtiers.[8]

107–112   4. Women spent hours practicing walking. The fashion for women at court was to wear tight corsets and large hoop skirts that were heavy and awkwardly sized, so moving about the palace was quite tricky. To make things more complicated, when they were introduced to the king, they would have to curtsy several times as they walked up to the throne and then repeat the whole thing in reverse on the way back. It was a sign of

---

[5] Setareh Janda, *Royal French Manners Were so Weird that You Could Pee Directly in Front of the Queen*, "Weird History".
[6] Setareh Janda, *Royal French Manners…*
[7] Aurora von Goeth, *Ten Rules of Etiquette for you Versailles Visit…*, "Party Like 1660".
[8] Setareh Janda.

Annotation Notes			Reading Notes

disrespect to turn one's back on royalty.[9] So, these women would have rehearsals for balls and dinners so as not to embarrass themselves.

5. Women would use fans to communicate complicated thoughts that were too rude to say out loud.

6. Higher ranking courtiers did not have to leave their beds to meet with lower-ranking courtiers.[10]

7. If a servant passed a noble with a meal for the king, the noble was expected to bow to the food.[11]

8. When conversing with someone, it was rude not to compliment them. Courtiers were expected to have compliments ready. It was inexcusable to use the same compliment on someone twice or to an acquaintance of someone they had already used the compliment on already.[12]

9. There was a proper way to use a napkin and how far to unfold it that changed depending on how high one's rank at court was.[13]

10. Gentlemen were required to wear formal attire and swords when they watched the king eat. If they forgot their sword, they could rent one for the evening. Additionally, how often a courtier could change their clothes and how many different outfits they had reflected how wealthy they were. Many women of the court would change their outfit by adding, changing, or removing a shawl, brooch, jewelry, or other such accessories.[14]

*Despite all these strict rules, there was no rule for proper hygiene etiquette. A courtier was not required to bathe, and because court clothes cost more than some courtiers made in a year, they often only had a couple of different outfits. Washing the clothes was also a challenge as many were so sensitive that washing would ruin them. Also, there were no rules about where a courtier could relieve themselves, and because there were so few public toilets in the palace (and they were often filthy), many courtiers would take advantage of this and would relieve themselves in public rooms.[15] For instance, Princess d'Harcourt would often relieve herself in the hallway without stopping what she was doing (much to the annoyance of the servants who had to clean up after her).[16] Foreign dignitaries often reported that while the Palace of Versailles was very lavish and elegantly decorated, it had a foul and permanent smell.

The Bourgeoisie

The *bourgeoisie* has two groups the *Haute Bourgeoisie* (upper-middle class) and the P*etite Bourgeoisie* (lower middle class). The upper-middle class was comprised mainly of highly educated and wealthy merchants, doctors, lawyers, and politicians. The lower middle class usually had some level of education and skill. These usually were store owners, professors or teachers, and skilled artisans. The more work someone did with the nobility (for example: selling furs and silks to nobility or treating the

I Wonder

I Notice

---

[9] Setareh Janda.
[10] Aurora von Goeth, *Ten Rules of Etiquette…*
[11] Ibid.
[12] *French Court Etiquette at Versailles and Who Was "Madame Etiquette"?,* "Etiquipedia", (Friday, Dec. 20, 2013).
[13] Aurora von Goeth.
[14] Ibid.
[15] Setareh Janda.
[16] John Pike, *"Nobility - Classes and Precedence,"* (Global Security org, 2011).

Annotation Notes		Reading Notes
	158 wounds of a nobleman), the more affluent and higher the 159 status of that person. 160 The *bourgeoisie* was a growing class in France due to 161 the growing world trade and expansion to the various 162 colonies. Many of the upper-middle class also had 163 ambitions to become part of the aristocracy. By buying 164 titled land (with permission of the king), they could obtain 165 this, though it was relatively rare, which led to a great deal 166 of discontent among the *bourgeoisie*. 167 It was the bourgeoisie that comprised the Third Estate 168 of the French government (see more in the government 169 section). 170 *The Prolétariat* 171 The *prolétariat*, or the working class, was comprised 172 primarily of fishermen, farmers, household servants, and 173 laborers. They were the largest of the social classes and, 174 while they were the poorest, they were also responsible for 175 paying most of the state's taxes. They also went 176 unrepresented in the government. 177 **The Government** 178 The French government consisted firstly of the king 179 and then of the Estates-General. The Estates-General was a 180 legislative (law-making) and consultative (providing advice 181 to the king) branch of the government that had three 182 different groups or "estates." The First Estate was made up 183 primarily of the clergy or religious class. The Second Estate 184 was made up of nobility, and the Third Estate was made up 185 of the commoners or the *bourgeoisie*. When an issue came 186 to a vote, and there was disagreement, the First and Second 187 Estates usually voted against the Third, even though the 188 Third Estate represented a majority of the population. This 189 created an imbalance among the classes and their 190 representation in the government. The Estates-General, 191 unlike the English Parliament, had no real power and would 192 only be called into session or dismissed by the king. They 193 functioned primarily as an advisory council to the king by 194 presenting petitions from the various estates and consulting 195 the king of fiscal matters.[17] 196 **The Economy**	I Wonder I Notice

[17] Hoge Raad van Adel (in Dutch), "Adeldom: Predikaat of Title," (Archived from the original on 23 April 2015. Retrieved 5 May 2015).

Annotation Notes			**Closing Impressions**

Closing Impressions

Central Ideas (CI) / Topic
Has your understanding of the CI/Topic Changed? If so, how? If not, provide an additional piece of textual evidence on the lines below to support your previous CI.

_____

_____

_____

Textual Evidence to support your CI (Use the page and line #s as a reference)

_____

_____

_____

_____

Author Bias
Does the author show bias toward any of the people groups mentioned?

_____

_____

_____

Textual Evidence (Use the page and line #s as a reference)

_____

_____

_____

197 At the start of the 17th century, France was in a great
198 deal of debt because of the French Wars of Religion.
199 However, King Henry IV began to institute several
200 monetary reforms to reduce the tax burden on the peasants
201 as well as the national debt. These policies continued under
202 Louis XIII; however, the country was still in a vast amount
203 of debt and turmoil when King Louis XIV took over in his
204 own right. King Louis XIV, in order to fund his two
205 expensive projects, military conquest and the Palace of
206 Versailles, instituted taxes on all French subjects, even the
207 nobles and the clergy. However, the nobles could buy their
208 way out of paying taxes with a large sum upfront. He also
209 promoted policies that increased the trade industry of
210 France, specifically in trade related to luxury goods,
211 making France the tastemaker of Europe.

212 Nevertheless, while France seemed to be in an
213 economic boom, it was also overly restrictive to the
214 working class. It discouraged innovation change, and high
215 taxes and tariffs supported it.

216 *Effects of the Protestant Emigration*

217 When the Louis XIV revoked the Edict of Nantes,
218 Protestants fled France, causing France to lose many
219 profitable, tax-paying business-owners and skilled artisans.
220 Some Protestants even took with them some of the Catholic
221 employees. The government then raised taxes in order to
222 support the lavish lifestyle of the nobility in Versailles.

Briefly Summarize the Passage (Use the back or a separate sheet of paper for more space)

Annotation Notes			First Impressions

223
224

The Dutch Republic: Society, Government, and Economy

225 **Social Class**

226 *Structure/Overview*

227 In the Netherlands, social status was not based on
228 etiquette or titles, but one's financial status; the more one
229 makes, the more respected and influential that person
230 became in society. Wealthy merchants could more
231 frequently buy their way into nobility than French nobles,
232 making class mobility much more flexible than in France.

233 *Titles*

234 Like in France, the Netherlands (also called **The**
235 **Dutch Republic** or the Republic of the Seven United
236 Netherlands) reserved titles for landed nobility only. Such
237 titles included: Prince – notice they did not have the title
238 "King" – Duke, Marquis, Count, Viscount, Baron, and
239 Knight. Those who are in the nobility class but did not have
240 a title (for instance, the child of a living titled Lord) would
241 carry the word *Jonkheer* before their name.[18]

242 Titles were most often passed down from father to son.
243 However, a Royal Decree could also grant a person a title,
244 and some noble immigrants could, with permission, bring
245 in their title from their homeland.

246 *The Clergy*

247 The clergy in the Netherlands played a minimal role in
248 society; they had neither the influence, power, or wealth of
249 their French counterparts. In the early 16th century
250 Catholicism was the primary religion when the Protestant
251 Reformation began to form. Lutheranism (the first branch
252 of Protestantism) had little effect in the Netherlands.
253 However, Calvinism just a few decades later spread quickly
254 through the country. At the time, the King of Spain and the
255 Netherlands, Phillip II, was a devout Catholic and felt it his
256 duty to fight Protestantism in his territory. Despite all his
257 efforts, Calvinism won out by converting both elite
258 officials as well as the general population. So, in 1648,
259 Spain and the Holy Roman Empire recognized the
260 independence of the Netherlands in the Treaty of
261 Westphalia. Now free from Catholic rule, the newly formed

First Impressions

Central Ideas (CI) / Topic
What is the CI/Topic?
_____
_____
_____

Textual Evidence (Use the page and line #s as a reference)
_____
_____
_____
_____

Purpose (POV)
**Circle ONE
- Entertain
- Persuade
- Inform

Textual Evidence (Use the page and line #s as a reference)
_____
_____
_____

---

[18] Jonathan Irvine Israel, *The Dutch Republic: Its Rise, Greatness, and Fall 1477-1806*, (1995).

Annotation Notes		Reading Notes
	Dutch Republic became a stronghold for Protestantism. Though the Netherlands maintained a Catholic area in order to promote religious toleration, the de facto state religion in most of the Seven Provinces was Calvinism.[19]	I Wonder
	There was not a separation of church and state as we recognize it today. However, religion in the Netherlands played a much smaller role in government than many of the surrounding countries.	
	The Aristocracy	
	The aristocracy also played a much smaller role in society than their counterparts in France, especially in Amsterdam, the hub of trade. Most nobles lived in the more undeveloped inland country, though several also kept houses in the more substantial trade cities. Few nobles had much, if any, influence in the country's most prominent industry: trade. However, the Dutch nobility maintained some significance in the government by forming knighthoods in each province and reserving certain offices for nobility only (see more in the government section).[20]	I Notice
	Unlike in France, the aristocrats in the Netherlands often mixed with other classes by marrying their daughters to wealthy merchants or even becoming traders themselves.	
	The Bourgeoisie	
	The wealthy merchant class, consisting of highly educated merchants (also known as **patricians**), became the real power in the Dutch Republic even before their emancipation from Spanish rule. The Dutch Provinces were continually criticizing for acting without permission of the throne.[21] After their independence from Spanish rule and the new Dutch Republic was formed, the Netherlands entered into what is called the **Dutch Golden Age** (more on this in the Economy section). During this period, trade was the principal industry of the nation, and the merchant class began to take over many positions in the new government as a way to increase their wealth and power. Many wealth merchants even purchased their way into nobility by buying land and coats of arms and seals, and many others married the daughters of nobles.	
	After the patricians, came the upper-middle class. This class consisted primarily of protestant ministers, lawyers,	

---

[19] Haley, Kenneth, Harold, Dobson, *The Dutch in the Seventeenth Century. Thames and Hudson,* (Oxford University Press, 1972), p. 78.
[20] Jonathan Israel, *The Dutch Republic.*
[21] *Haley, Kenneth, Harold, Dobson,* The Dutch in the Seventeenth Century.

Annotation Notes			Reading Notes

302 doctors, small merchants. In contrast, the lower middle
303 class consisted of farmers, craft and tradesmen, shop
304 owners, or low government officers/bureaucrats.

I Wonder

305 *The Prolétariat*

306 The lower classes consisted of skilled laborers, maids,
307 servants, sailors, and other service industry workers. It is
308 interesting to note that workers and laborers, while still
309 relatively low in society, were generally paid much better
310 than in other countries and experienced much higher living
311 standards than their counterparts in France. However,
312 despite these improvements, the working class also had to
313 pay higher than average taxes.

314 **The Government**

315 After the emancipation of the Netherlands from
316 Spanish control, the new Dutch Republic developed a
317 rather complicated government: this consisted of a national
318 branch, seven state or province branches, as well as
319 governments for each city. Instead of relying on a king, the
320 Dutch Republic had a body of representatives called
321 **regents** that voted on national and regional decisions.
322 These regents were not voted in by the public the same way
323 we vote in the United States today. Instead, the regents
324 were made up of patricians (wealthy merchants), and these
325 government positions were often "reserved" as life-long
326 positions.[22] It is interesting to note that despite less
327 emphasis on religion in the government and the country's
328 promotion of religious tolerance, government officials were
329 still required to be Calvinists.

I Notice

330 The National Government of the Dutch Republic was
331 led primarily by the following two branches:

332 • The States-General (or the Generality)
333 They were in charge of conducting foreign
334 relations, declaring war and peace, administered
335 the army and navy, and levied taxes.[23]
336 • The Council of State
337 This was a sub-committee of the States-General
338 in charge of executing or enforcing the decisions
339 of the Generality.

340 In addition to these two, there was also the admiralties
341 (in charge of the navy administration and affairs), and the

---

[22] Sir William Temple, *Observations upon the United Provinces of the Netherlands (7th ed.)*, "London: Jacob Tonfon within Grays-Inn Gate next Grays-Inn Lane, and Awnfoam and John Churchill at the Black Swan in Tater-No/ler-Row."
[23] Jonathan I. Israel.

Annotation Notes			Reading Notes
			I Wonder

342 chartered companies Dutch East India Trading Company
343 and the Dutch West Trading Company.

344   The Delegated Councilors led the Province
345 government. They consisted of one representative from the
346 nobility, one from each of the seven largest cities, and one
347 from the three smaller towns.[24] There was also the
348 Councilor Pensionary, a position that had a five-year term,
349 was paid a salary and was in charge of studying, proposing,
350 and carrying out the decisions of the province.[25] It also
351 included a position called the stadtholder, a life-long
352 position for nobles only. While the stadtholder had much
353 less power than the other branches, they could indirectly
354 influence the general policy overtime.

355   The most important stadtholder was the title of Prince
356 of Oranges, the stadtholder of the province of Holland. It
357 was customary for ambassadors of other countries to stop
358 by and discuss affairs with the Prince of Orange as well as
359 the States-General. The Prince of Orange was most

I Notice

360 influential during war-time as he was appointed both
361 Captain-General of the army and the Admiral-General of
362 the navy. Additionally, the Prince of Orange would preside
363 at the Council of State meetings. The title Prince of Orange
364 was the highest title awarded in the Netherlands, but unlike
365 the King of France, the Prince of Orange was an advisory
366 position only.[26]

367 **The Economy**

368   At the time that Etienne and his family traveled to
369 Amsterdam, the Netherlands was experiencing an
370 economic boom that was later called the Dutch Golden
371 Age. Amsterdam was the hub of this economic boom as it
372 was the center for world trade.[27] All types of luxury goods
373 ended up in Amsterdam for sorting, processing, and
374 distribution to other parts of the world, including what is
375 now called the Americas.[28]

376   The trade was so great that the Dutch ended up
377 building the largest merchant fleet in the world up to that
378 date. They were also leading innovations in technologies
379 such as the sawmill and wind-powered mechanization.

---

[24] Petrus Johannes Blok, *History of the people of the Netherlands* (New York: G. P. Putnam's Sons, 1898).
[25] Rowen, Herbert H, *The princes of Orange: the stadtholders in the Dutch Republic*, (Cambridge University Press, 1988), p.29.
[26] Charles R. Boxer, *The Dutch Seaborne Empire 1600–1800*, (Oxford, Clarendon Press, 1965).
[27] Joost Jonker, *Merchants, bankers, middlemen: the Amsterdam money market during the first half of the 19th century*, (NEHA, 1996), p. 32.
[28] "1637 Tulipmania," *Timeline Dutch History – Rijksstudio*, (Rijksmuseum).

Annotation Notes			Reading Notes
	380	**Fun Fact: Tulipmania**	
	381	Tulips, which came from Turkey, were introduced in the 16th	I Wonder
	382	century. The exotic flower was bred into a variety of colors, both solid	
	383	and variegated, with smooth and frilled petals. Breeders keep	
	384	meticulous records of the various species. The flowers were so	
	385	desirable that potters designed unique vases for them. Limited varieties	
	386	became so expensive that people began to trade them on the stock	
	387	exchange, and investors began to speculate on the rarest species. Many	
	388	economic scholars considered this the first **speculative bubble**, trade in	
	389	an asset where the cost far exceeds the actual value, in history. Many	
	390	people jumped onto the opportunity, even putting up their homes as	
	391	collateral. Then the prices suddenly plummeted in February 1637,	
	392	leaving many investors penniless.[29] Tulips continued to be a key part of	
	393	Dutch culture and society.	
	394	*The Dutch East and West India Trading Companies*	
	395	There were two major joint-stock companies in	
	396	Amsterdam: The United East India Company (VOC); and	
	397	the West Indies Company (WIC). The VOC was	
	398	established March 20, 1602, to trade with Mughal India and	I Notice
	399	in the Southeast Asian spice trade. While the WIC received	
	400	its charter on June 3, 1621, from the Republic of the Seven	
	401	United Netherlands, for a trade monopoly to participate in	
	402	the Atlantic slave trade, Brazil, the Caribbean, and North	
	403	America.	
	404	The VOC is considered by many to be the forerunner	
	405	of the modern international corporation today. From its	
	406	beginning, it was created to be not only a commercial	
	407	venture but also to fulfill a military role in the global trade	
	408	wars with Spain and Portugal. The VOC also launched the	
	409	first formal stock exchange in Amsterdam in 1611.	
	410	The West Indies Company was established much like	
	411	the East India Company, though it was not as successful.	
	412	Unlike the VOC, the WIC was not authorized to use	
	413	military force, as a result of signing the Treaty of	
	414	Westphalia in October of 1648. The company's initial goal	
	415	was to carry slaves from Africa and sugar from Brazil. The	
	416	company's initial ventures proved to be too expensive and	
	417	did not yield the expected profit due to intense competition	
	418	with Portugal.[30] The WIC only stayed in business as a	
	419	result of obtaining a monopoly to trade in gold and African	
	420	slaves in 1649. By 1663 and 1664, they were selling more	
	421	enslaved Africans than the Portuguese and English	
	422	together.	

---

[29] Charles R. Boxer, *The Dutch in Brazil 1624 - 1654*. (Oxford, Clarendon Press, 1957).
[30] John Mark Reynolds, *Ten Reasons for Calvinists to Be Cheerful this Christmas*, (First Things, 12/5/09)

Annotation Notes			Closing Impressions

The Effects of the Protestant Immigration

423
424 Calvinists, more formally called, Reformists, like the
425 French Huguenots, believed that because people should be
426 capable of reading the Bible for themselves without
427 interpretation from the priests. As a result, they supported
428 public education for their children. Religious education was
429 essential to ensure that their children knew the fundamental
430 Christian beliefs. Arithmetic was also crucial since most
431 were merchants, bankers, or tradesmen. Because of their
432 emphasis on education, when the protestants fled to
433 Amsterdam, they brought with them a wealth of knowledge
434 and diversity. Many scholars believe this helped to make
435 the Dutch Golden Age so profitable.

Fun Fact: Christmas

437 In the 17th century, Reformists (aka Calvinists, like Huguenots,
438 Pilgrims, and Puritans) did not encourage the celebration of Christmas
439 for several reasons. Firstly, they argued, Christmas was more closely
440 associated with pagan practices because Catholics wanted to hide their
441 celebrations from the secular government so as not to be persecuted.
442 Secondly, there was no tradition in the Bible or early Church of
443 observing Jesus's birth as a holiday. Thirdly, Reformers did not like the
444 excessive partying and drinking that was always associated with
445 Christmas.[31]

446 The Scottish Presbyterians were the first to ban Christmas in
447 1560.[32] Oliver Cromwell banned it in England in 1644 and did not
448 bring it back until 1660.[33] In Amsterdam in the 17th century,
449 gingerbread men and women were not allowed to be sold. Pilgrim's
450 when they first arrived in the New World did not recognize Christmas,
451 continuing to work in the fields on that day. Massachusetts Bay colony
452 also banned the celebration of Christmas as a Popish celebration in
453 1659 and did not reinstate it until 1681.[34]

Closing Impressions

Central Ideas (CI) / Topic
Has your understanding of the CI/Topic Changed? If so, how? If not, provide an additional piece of textual evidence on the lines below to support your previous CI.

Textual Evidence to support your CI (Use the page and line #s as a reference)

Author Bias
Does the author show bias toward any of the people groups mentioned?

Textual Evidence (Use the page and line #s as a reference)

Briefly Summarize the Passage (Use the back or a separate sheet of paper for more space)

---

[31] *Celebrating Christmas*, (Presbyterian Heritage Center, 2011).
[32] Paul Flesher, *Banned Christmas*, (Religion Today, 12/7/2010).
[33] C. Danko, "Once Upon a Time When Christmas Was Banned ...", *A Puritan's Mind*, (Puritans Publications, 1996-2019).
[34] Ibid.

Name _____

Class _____

Date _____

Teacher's Section!!

Claim: _____

Evidence: _____

Organization: _____

Language: _____

Total Score: _____

Historical Background for
Thrown to the Wind Part 2
France: Society, Government, and Economics

Social Class

Structure/Overview

French social class structure in the 17th century was rigid and complicated. There was little to no social mobility between the four primary classes: The Catholic clergy (cardinals and bishops), the aristocracy (the nobility), the *bourgeoisie* (the middle class), and the *prolétariat* (the lower class).

Titles

The nobility were the only people honored with titles. Whereas today we might address someone as sir, ma'am, mister (Mr.), misses (Mrs.), or miss (Ms.) these used to be titles reserved for English nobility only. Likewise, France had similar titles for their nobility. These titles were passed down from father to son when the father passed away. In a few French regions that had previously been independent before France conquered them, there were a few titles passed down the female line, but this was rare.

The king and his family had even more complicated titles. Formally, he would be presented to the room as "The King His Most Christian Majesty." If addressed directly by another royal the first time, they would call him "The King Your Most Christian Majesty." Every time after the first introduction, he could be called "Your/His Majesty," "Sire," or "Monsieur le Roi." Whereas the king and queen were addressed with the title "Your Majesty," the princes and princesses would be addressed as "Your Highness."[12]

Other French nobility would be addressed as Monsieur, Madame, or Mademoiselle, unless the king's brother and wife were present. More formally, they would be called by their first name, followed by "de" and the name of their house of property.

The *bourgeoisie* and *prolétariat* did not have titles, though teachers were called *maistre*, as a form of respect. Among the Protestants, the title of "Brother" was often used as a form of association. Additionally, the term "Goodwife" was frequently used to refer to a married woman.

It is interesting to note that, in France, it was generally impolite to call people by name in their presence. One knew who was being addressed by the use of eye contact. Names were used only when the person was not present or in order to get someone's attention when eye contact was not possible. Additionally, nicknames were seldom used in 17th century France.

The Catholic Clergy

The Catholic Clergy was at the top of the social structure along with the nobility. They played such an important role in French society that they even dominated a whole branch of the French government called The First Estate (more on this in the government section). Many of these bishops and clergymen "considered themselves socially, intellectually, and morally superior to other members of [the government and] held that the First Estate should maintain its independence and have a broader role in government and society."[13]

---

[12] "The Art of Addressing French Nobility," *Party Like 1660*.

[13] J. Michael Hayden and Malcolm R. Greenshields, *French Historical Studies*: "The Clergy of Early Seventeenth Century France: Self-Perception and

The Catholic Clergy, much like the government, had a hierarchy or ranking system that puts some people over others as more respected, wealthier, and more powerful.

The highest authority in the Church belongs to the Bishop of Rome, the Pope, who "has full, supreme and universal power over the whole church, a power which he can always exercise unhindered."[14]

After the Pope, the order goes:[15]

- Cardinals
- Archbishops
- Bishops
- Priests
- Deacons
- Laity

The Aristocracy

The aristocracy was among the top of society. In addition to dominating the Second Estate of the government, the aristocracy had many specific legal and financial privileges. Among all French citizens, they were the only ones allowed to hunt, to wear a sword, and to own land or hold certain military, civic, or clerical positions. Additionally, they were exempt from the *taille* or tax. They could also issue additional taxes on those who lived and worked on their land.

Nobles were required to swear loyalty to the king and often had to serve in the military or pay a "blood tax" to support the military. Additionally, the king could revoke a noble's title if they engaged in specific tasks like manual labor.[16]

Fun Fact: Silly Court Rules

King Louis XIV's (The Sun King) court of nobles in Versailles was full of precise rules or etiquette that determined one's status in court. How well a noble could follow all the rules largely determined their rank and status among the other nobles. Here are some of the weirdest rules.

1. Knocking with one's knuckles on a door was impolite. Instead, courtiers were expected to lightly scratch on the door frame as a way to announce their presence. As a result, many courtiers grew out one of their nails to use for this purpose.[17]
2. Every part of the king's daily tasks were on display to nobles, including getting up in the morning, washing up, dressing and undressing, eating, and even using the toilet. The king would grant courtiers with special favor the honor of handing the king his shirt as he dressed or a special place close to him while he sat on the toilet.[18]
3. Only some people had the right to sit. The King and Queen would sit in a cushioned armchair. Close relatives of the king, such as his brother or sons and daughters, would be allowed to sit in an armless chair. Lastly, duchesses would be allowed to sit on stools. Everyone else would have to stand. Furthermore, a noble had to be invited to sit by a higher ranking official. So, even if one was of rank, they could be denied a seat if they insulted the higher-ranking courtiers.[19]
4. Women spent hours practicing how to walk. The fashion for women at court was to wear tight corsets and large hoop skirts that were heavy and awkwardly sized, so moving about the palace was quite tricky. To make things more complicated, when they were introduced to the king, they would have to curtsy several times as they walked up to the throne and then repeat the whole thing in reverse on the way back. It was a sign of disrespect to turn one's back on royalty.[20] So, these women would have rehearsals for balls and dinners so as not to embarrass themselves.

Society's Perception." Vol. 18, No. 1 (Spring, 1993), pp. 145-172

[14] *Catechism of the Catholic Church*, no.882.

[15] CE Editors, *Explaining the Hierarchy of the Church*. Catholic Exchange. Feb. 17th, 2005.

[16] Setareh Janda, *Royal French Manners Were so Weird that You Could Pee Directly in Front of the Queen*, "Weird History".

[17] Setareh Janda, *Royal French Manners…*

[18] Aurora von Goeth, *Ten Rules of Etiquette for you Versailles Visit…*, "Party Like 1660".

[19] Setareh Janda.

[20] Ibid.

5. Women would use fans to communicate complicated thoughts that were too rude to say out loud.
6. Higher ranking courtiers did not have to leave their beds to meet with lower-ranking courtiers.[21]
7. If a servant passed a noble with a meal for the king, the noble was expected to bow to the food.[22]
8. When conversing with someone, it was rude not to compliment them. Courtiers were expected to have compliments ready. It was inexcusable to use the same compliment on someone twice or to an acquaintance of someone they had already used the compliment on already.[23]
9. There was a proper way to use a napkin and how far to unfold it that changed depending on how high one's rank at court was.[24]
10. Gentlemen were required to wear formal attire and swords when they watched the king eat. If they forgot their sword, they could rent one for the evening. Additionally, how often a courtier could change their clothes and how many different outfits they had reflected how wealthy they were. Many women of the court would change their outfit by adding, changing, or removing a shawl, brooch, jewelry, or other such accessories.[25]

*Despite all these strict rules, there was no rule for proper hygiene etiquette. A courtier was not required to bathe, and because court clothes cost more than some courtiers made in a year, they often only had a couple of different outfits. Washing the clothes was also a challenge as many were so sensitive that washing would ruin them. Also, there were no rules about where a courtier could relieve themselves, and because there were so few public toilets in the palace (and they were often filthy), many courtiers would take advantage of this and would relieve themselves in public rooms.[26] For instance, Princess d'Harcourt would often relieve herself in the hallway without stopping what she was doing (much to the annoyance of the servants who had to clean up after her).[27] Foreign dignitaries often reported that while the Palace of Versailles was very lavish and elegantly decorated, it had a foul and permanent smell.

The Bourgeoisie

The *bourgeoisie* has two groups the *Haute Bourgeoisie* (upper-middle class) and the *Petite Bourgeoisie* (lower middle class). The upper-middle class was comprised mainly of highly educated and wealthy merchants, doctors, lawyers, and politicians. The lower middle class usually had some level of education and skill. These usually were store owners, professors or teachers, and skilled artisans. The more work someone did with the nobility (for example: selling furs and silks to nobility or treating the wounds of a nobleman), the more affluent and higher the status of that person.

The *bourgeoisie* was a growing class in France due to the growing world trade and expansion to the various colonies. Many of the upper-middle class also had ambitions to become part of the aristocracy. By buying titled land (with permission of the king), they could obtain this, though it was relatively rare, which led to a great deal of discontent among the *bourgeoisie*.

It was the bourgeoisie that comprised the Third Estate of the French government (see more in the government section).

The Prolétariat

The *prolétariat*, or the working class, was comprised primarily of fishermen, farmers, household servants, and laborers. They were the largest of the social classes and, while they were the poorest, they were also responsible for paying most of the state's taxes. They also went unrepresented in the government.

The Government

The French government consisted firstly of the king and then of the Estates-General. The Estates-General was a legislative (law-making) and consultative (providing advice to the king) branch of the government that had three different groups or "estates." The First Estate was made up primarily of the clergy or religious class. The Second Estate was made up of nobility, and the

---

[21] Aurora von Goeth, *Ten Rules of Etiquette…*
[22] Ibid.
[23] *French Court Etiquette at Versailles and Who Was "Madame Etiquette"?*, "Etiquipedia", (Friday, Dec. 20, 2013).
[24] Aurora von Goeth.
[25] Ibid.
[26] Setareh Janda.
[27] John Pike, *"Nobility - Classes and Precedence,"* (Global Security org, 2011).

Third Estate was made up of the commoners or the *bourgeoisie*. When an issue came to a vote, and there was disagreement, the First and Second Estates usually voted against the Third, even though the Third Estate represented a majority of the population. This created an imbalance among the classes and their representation in the government. The Estates-General, unlike the English Parliament, had no real power and would only be called into session or dismissed by the king. They functioned primarily as an advisory council to the king by presenting petitions from the various estates and consulting the king of fiscal matters.[28]

The Economy

At the start of the 17th century, France was in a great deal of debt because of the French Wars of Religion. However, King Henry IV began to institute several monetary reforms to reduce the tax burden on the peasants as well as the national debt. These policies continued under Louis XIII; however, the country was still in a vast amount of debt and turmoil when King Louis XIV took over in his own right. King Louis XIV, in order to fund his two expensive projects, military conquest and the Palace of Versailles, instituted taxes on all French subjects, even the nobles and the clergy. However, the nobles could buy their way out of paying taxes with a large sum upfront. He also promoted policies that increased the trade industry of France, specifically in trade related to luxury goods, making France the tastemaker of Europe.

Nevertheless, while France seemed to be in an economic boom, it was also overly restrictive to the working class. It discouraged innovation change, and high taxes and tariffs supported it.

Effects of the Protestant Emigration

When the Louis XIV revoked the Edict of Nantes, Protestants fled France, causing France to lose many profitable, tax-paying business-owners and skilled artisans. Some Protestants even took with them some of the Catholic employees. The government then raised taxes in order to support the lavish lifestyle of the nobility in Versailles.

Vue de port de La Rochelle, by Ambroise-Louis Gameray (1783-1857)
Bibliothèque et Archives, Canada
Common Domain

---

[28] Hoge Raad van Adel (in Dutch), "Adeldom: Predikaat of Title," (Archived from the original on 23 April 2015. Retrieved 5 May 2015).

Name _____ Class _____ Date _____

The Dutch Republic: Society, Government, and Economy

Social Class

Structure/Overview

In the Netherlands, social status was not based on etiquette or titles, but one's financial status; the more one makes, the more respected and influential that person became in society. Wealthy merchants could more frequently buy their way into nobility than French nobles, making class mobility much more flexible than in France.

Titles

Like in France, the Netherlands (also called **The Dutch Republic** or the Republic of the Seven United Netherlands) reserved titles for landed nobility only. Such titles included: Prince – notice they did not have the title "King" – Duke, Marquis, Count, Viscount, Baron, and Knight. Those who are in the nobility class but did not have a title (for instance, the child of a living titled Lord) would carry the word *Jonkheer* before their name.[29]

Titles were most often passed down from father to son. However, a Royal Decree could also grant a person a title, and some noble immigrants could, with permission, bring in their title from their homeland.

The Clergy

The clergy in the Netherlands played a minimal role in society; they had neither the influence, power, or wealth of their French counterparts. In the early 16th century Catholicism was the primary religion when the Protestant Reformation began to form. Lutheranism (the first branch of Protestantism) had little effect in the Netherlands. However, Calvinism just a few decades later spread quickly through the country. At the time, the King of Spain and the Netherlands, Phillip II, was a devout Catholic and felt it his duty to fight Protestantism in his territory. Despite all his efforts, Calvinism won out by converting both elite officials as well as the general population. So, in 1648, Spain and the Holy Roman Empire recognized the independence of the Netherlands in the Treaty of Westphalia. Now free from Catholic rule, the newly formed Dutch Republic became a stronghold for Protestantism. Though the Netherlands maintained a Catholic area in order to promote religious toleration, the de facto state religion in most of the Seven Provinces was Calvinism.[30]

There was not a separation of church and state as we recognize it today. However, religion in the Netherlands played a much smaller role in government than many of the surrounding countries.

The Aristocracy

The aristocracy also played a much smaller role in society than their counterparts in France, especially in Amsterdam, the hub of trade. Most nobles lived in the more undeveloped inland country, though several also kept houses in the more substantial trade cities. Few nobles had much, if any, influence in the country's most prominent industry: trade. However, the Dutch nobility maintained some significance in the government by forming knighthoods in each province and reserving certain offices for nobility only (see more in the government section).[31]

Unlike in France, the aristocrats in the Netherlands often mixed with other classes by marrying their daughters to wealthy merchants or even becoming traders themselves.

The Bourgeoisie

The wealthy merchant class, consisting of highly educated merchants (also known as **patricians**), became the real power in the Dutch Republic even before their emancipation from Spanish rule. The Dutch Provinces were continually criticizing for acting without

---

[29] Jonathan Irvine Israel, *The Dutch Republic: Its Rise, Greatness, and Fall 1477-1806*, (1995).

[30] Haley, Kenneth, Harold, Dobson, *The Dutch in the Seventeenth Century*. Thames and Hudson, (Oxford University Press, 1972), p. 78.

[31] Jonathan Israel, *The Dutch Republic*.

permission of the throne.[32] After their independence from Spanish rule and the new Dutch Republic was formed, the Netherlands entered into what is called the **Dutch Golden Age** (more on this in the Economy section). During this period, trade was the principal industry of the nation, and the merchant class began to take over many positions in the new government as a way to increase their wealth and power. Many wealth merchants even purchased their way into nobility by buying land and coats of arms and seals, and many others married the daughters of nobles.

After the patricians, came the upper-middle class. This class consisted primarily of protestant ministers, lawyers, doctors, small merchants. In contrast, the lower middle class consisted of farmers, craft and tradesmen, shop owners, or low government officers/bureaucrats.

The Prolétariat

The lower classes consisted of skilled laborers, maids, servants, sailors, and other service industry workers. It is interesting to note that workers and laborers, while still relatively low in society, were generally paid much better than in other countries and experienced much higher living standards than their counterparts in France. However, despite these improvements, the working class also had to pay higher than average taxes.

The Government

After the emancipation of the Netherlands from Spanish control, the new Dutch Republic developed a rather complicated government: this consisted of a national branch, seven state or province branches, as well as governments for each city. Instead of relying on a king, the Dutch Republic had a body of representatives called **regents** that voted on national and regional decisions. These regents were not voted in by the public the same way we vote in the United States today. Instead, the regents were made up of patricians (wealthy merchants), and these government positions were often "reserved" as life-long positions.[33] It is interesting to note that despite less emphasis on religion in the government and the country's promotion of religious tolerance, government officials were still required to be Calvinists.

The National Government of the Dutch Republic was led primarily by the following two branches:

- The States-General (or the Generality)
  They were in charge of conducting foreign relations, declaring war and peace, administered the army and navy, and levied taxes.[34]
- The Council of State
  This was a sub-committee of the States-General in charge of executing or enforcing the decisions of the Generality.

In addition to these two, there was also the admiralties (in charge of the navy administration and affairs), and the chartered companies Dutch East India Trading Company and the Dutch West Trading Company.

The Delegated Councilors led the Province government. They consisted of one representative from the nobility, one from each of the seven largest cities, and one from the three smaller towns.[35] There was also the Councilor Pensionary, a position that had a five-year term, was paid a salary and was in charge of studying, proposing, and carrying out the decisions of the province.[36] It also included a position called the stadtholder, a life-long position for nobles only. While the stadtholder had much less power than the other branches, they could indirectly influence the general policy overtime.

The most important stadtholder was the title of Prince of Oranges, the stadtholder of the province of Holland. It was customary for ambassadors of other countries to stop by and discuss affairs with the Prince of Orange as well as the States-General. The Prince of Orange was most

---

[32] *Haley, Kenneth, Harold, Dobson,* The Dutch in the Seventeenth Century.
[33] Sir William Temple, *Observations upon the United Provinces of the Netherlands (7th ed.),* "London: Jacob Tonfon within Grays-Inn Gate next Grays-Inn Lane, and Awnfoam and John Churchill at the Black Swan in Tater-No/ler-Row."
[34] Jonathan I. Israel.
[35] Petrus Johannes Blok, *History of the people of the Netherlands* (New York: G. P. Putnam's Sons, 1898).
[36] Rowen, Herbert H, *The princes of Orange: the stadtholders in the Dutch Republic,* (Cambridge University Press, 1988), p.29.

influential during wartime as he was appointed both Captain-General of the army and the Admiral-General of the navy. Additionally, the Prince of Orange would preside at the Council of State meetings. The title Prince of Orange was the highest title awarded in the Netherlands, but unlike the King of France, the Prince of Orange was an advisory position only.[37]

The Economy

At the time that Etienne and his family traveled to Amsterdam, the Netherlands was experiencing an economic boom that was later called the Dutch Golden Age. Amsterdam was the hub of this economic boom as it was the center for world trade.[38] All types of luxury goods ended up in Amsterdam for sorting, processing, and distribution to other parts of the world, including what is now called the Americas.[39]

The trade was so great that the Dutch ended up building the largest merchant fleet in the world up to that date. They were also leading innovations in technologies such as the sawmill and wind-powered mechanization.

Fun Fact: Tulipmania

Tulips, which came from Turkey, were introduced in the 16th century. The exotic flower was bred into a variety of colors, both solid and variegated, with smooth and frilled petals. Breeders keep meticulous records of the various species. The flowers were so desirable that potters designed unique vases for them. Limited varieties became so expensive that people began to trade them on the stock exchange, and investors began to speculate on the rarest species. Many economic scholars considered this the first **speculative bubble**, trade in an asset where the cost far exceeds the actual value, in history. Many people jumped onto the opportunity, even putting up their homes as collateral. Then the prices suddenly plummeted in February 1637, leaving many investors penniless.[40] Tulips continued to be a key part of Dutch culture and society.

The Dutch East and West India Trading Companies

There were two major joint-stock companies in Amsterdam: The United East India Company (VOC); and the West Indies Company (WIC). The VOC was established March 20, 1602, to trade with Mughal India and in the Southeast Asian spice trade. While the WIC received its charter on June 3, 1621, from the Republic of the Seven United Netherlands, for a trade monopoly to participate in the Atlantic slave trade, Brazil, the Caribbean, and North America.

The VOC is considered by many to be the forerunner of the modern international corporation today. From its beginning, it was created to be not only a commercial venture but also to fulfill a military role in the global trade wars with Spain and Portugal. The VOC also launched the first formal stock exchange in Amsterdam in 1611.

The West Indies Company was established much like the East India Company, though it was not as successful. Unlike the VOC, the WIC was not authorized to use military force, as a result of signing the Treaty of Westphalia in October of 1648. The company's initial goal was to carry slaves from Africa and sugar from Brazil. The company's initial ventures proved to be too expensive and did not yield the expected profit due to intense competition with Portugal.[41] The WIC only stayed in business as a result of obtaining a monopoly to trade in gold and African slaves in 1649. By 1663 and 1664, they were selling more enslaved Africans than the Portuguese and English together.

---

[37] Charles R. Boxer, *The Dutch Seaborne Empire 1600–1800,* (Oxford, Clarendon Press, 1965).
[38] Joost Jonker, *Merchants, bankers, middlemen: the Amsterdam money market during the first half of the 19th century,* (NEHA, 1996), p. 32.
[39] "1637 Tulipmania," *Timeline Dutch History – Rijksstudio,* (Rijksmuseum).

[40] Charles R. Boxer, *The Dutch in Brazil 1624 - 1654.* (Oxford, Clarendon Press, 1957).
[41] John Mark Reynolds, *Ten Reasons for Calvinists to Be Cheerful this Christmas,* (First Things, 12/5/09)

The Effects of the Protestant Immigration

Calvinists, more formally called, Reformists, like the French Huguenots, believed that because people should be capable of reading the Bible for themselves without interpretation from the priests. As a result, they supported public education for their children. Religious education was essential to ensure that their children knew the fundamental Christian beliefs. Arithmetic was also crucial since most were merchants, bankers, or tradesmen. Because of their emphasis on education, when the protestants fled to Amsterdam, they brought with them a wealth of knowledge and diversity. Many scholars believe this helped to make the Dutch Golden Age so profitable.

Fun Fact: Christmas

In the 17th century, Reformists (aka Calvinists, like Huguenots, Pilgrims, and Puritans) did not encourage the celebration of Christmas for several reasons. Firstly, they argued, Christmas was more closely associated with pagan practices because Catholics wanted to hide their celebrations from the secular government so as not to be persecuted. Secondly, there was no tradition in the Bible or early Church of observing Jesus's birth as a holiday. Thirdly, Reformers did not like the excessive partying and drinking that was always associated with Christmas.[42]

The Scottish Presbyterians were the first to ban Christmas in 1560.[43] Oliver Cromwell banned it in England in 1644 and did not bring it back until 1660.[44] In Amsterdam in the 17th century, gingerbread men and women were not allowed to be sold. Pilgrim's when they first arrived in the New World did not recognize Christmas, continuing to work in the fields on that day. Massachusetts Bay colony also banned the celebration of Christmas as a Popish celebration in 1659 and did not reinstate it until 1681.[45]

Dam Square with the New Town Hall under Construction by Johannes Lingelbach, 1656

---

[42] *Celebrating Christmas*, (Presbyterian Heritage Center, 2011).
[43] Paul Flesher, *Banned Christmas*, (Religion Today, 12/7/2010).
[44] C. Danko, "Once Upon a Time When Christmas Was Banned ...", *A Puritan's Mind*, (Puritans Publications, 1996-2019).
[45] Ibid.

Amsterdam Museum

Group Activity (Teacher Resource)
Compare and Contrast: France and The Netherlands

Teacher Instructions: This is a 2 or 3-day activity where students will research, discuss, compare, and share what they have learned about the seventeenth century countries of France and The New Netherlands.

Day 1

1. Vocabulary Assignment: Underline all the words that appear to be technical history terms (Scaffolded: Use the highlighted words). Whether or not you are already familiar with the word, read the context around the word to create develop a guess definition for the word. After that, look up the word in the dictionary and write the exact, relevant definition(s) below your guess.

2. Assign student groups a culture (France or Netherlands) and a topic (social class, economy, government, or [advanced] religion).

3. Ask students to review the questions below the comparison chart, in order to think about the type of information they will need to fully answer the question.

4. Students will research their culture and topics starting with reviewing the information provided in the historical summary. Then they should continue their research on the web using the credible source checklist available in Appendix A (or for scaffolded provide additional resources).

5. Students should list the important characteristics of their topic and region on the comparison chart.

Day 2

1. Divide up the groups from Day 1 so that each new group contains at least one person representing each region for a given topic. For example, if Group 1 was researching French society and Group 2 was researching Dutch Society, the teacher would split these two groups and move ½ the Group 1 members to go work with the other ½ of Group 2, and vice versa.

2. Students then will share the information they researched on day one and will complete the comparison chart with the information provided from the remaining group members for their topic. For scaffolded or differentiated learning, the teacher may develop new groups that are centered on only one topic (this will then become a three-day activity).

3. Students in the group should answer the questions for their topic, comparing and contrasting the two cultures. Students may discuss their answers within the group, but the teacher should circulate the room to ensure that each student is contributing.

    a. Social
        i. What are the most significant differences?
        ii. What are the most significant similarities?

iii. How did the Huguenot immigration/emigration change or affect this aspect of society?

iv. *[If do not have Religion topic group]* How did religion play a role in this aspect of society?

b. Economy

i. What are the most significant differences and effects?

ii. What are the most significant similarities and effects?

iii. Did, and, if so, how did Huguenot immigration/emigration change or affect this aspect of society?

iv. [If do not have Religion topic group] How did religion play a role in this aspect of society?

c. Government

i. What were the most significant differences and effects?

ii. What were the most significant similarities and effects?

iii. Did, and, if so, how did Huguenot immigration/emigration change or affect this aspect of society?

iv. [If do not have Religion topic group] How did religion play a role in this aspect of society?

d. Religion *[Advanced groups only, as it requires being able to look at entire text not merely one section]*

i. How did religion play a role in social class in both: similarities and differences?

ii. How did religion play a role in government in both: similarities and differences?

iii. How did religion play a role in economics in both: similarities and differences?

Day 2, cont. or (scaffolded) Day 3

1. Now change up topic groups bringing one representative/scholar/expert from each topic and making new groups with one representative from each topic, so that each group has at least one representative from each topic.

2. Students will then teach their new group about their topic, while the other members of the group complete their comparison charts.

3. Students should then discuss the questions for each topic among the group. Teacher should stress that all students should have all of the areas in the comparison chart completed and all of the questions answered by the end of class (or to turn in the next day depending on available time).

4. Class discussion:

   a. First: groups decide upon a representative (scaffolded) or teacher chooses a representative.

   b. Second: the teacher asks random questions from the list to each group representative to check for comprehension and ensure all students hear all answers.

Name _____ Class _____ Date _____

Compare and Contrast: France and The Netherlands

Research your assigned culture and topic and list the important characteristics of your topic and complete your portion of the comparison chart.

	France	**Netherlands**
Social		
Economy		

www.windyseapublishing.com   *Windy Sea Publishing, LLC*   *Thrown to the Wind Teacher's Resource*

Government		
Religion		

Compare and contrast France and the Netherlands in the area assigned.
1. **Social**
   a. What are the most significant differences?

   b. What are the most significant similarities?

c. How did the Huguenot immigration/emigration change or affect this aspect of society?

d. *[If do not have Religion topic group]* How did religion play a role in this aspect of society?

2. **Economy**
   a. What are the most significant differences and effects?

   b. What are the most significant similarities and effects?

   c. Did, and, if so, how did Huguenot immigration/emigration change or affect this aspect of society?

   d. *[If do not have Religion topic group]* How did religion play a role in this aspect of society?

3. **Government**
   a. What were the most significant differences and effects?

   b. What were the most significant similarities and effects?

c. Did, and, if so, how did Huguenot immigration/emigration change or affect this aspect of society?

d. [If do not have Religion topic group] How did religion play a role in this aspect of society?

4. **Religion** *[Advanced groups only, as it requires being able to look at entire text not merely one section]*

   a. How did religion play a role in social class in both: similarities and differences?

   b. How did religion play a role in government in both: similarities and differences?

   c. How did religion play a role in economics in both: similarities and differences?

Name _____

Class _____

Date _____

Teacher's Section!!

Claim: _____

Evidence: _____

Organization: _____

Language: _____

Total Score: _____

Essay Prompt

Compare and Contrast: France and Netherlands

Student Instructions: Write an essay answering the following prompt. Be prepared to discuss it with the class. Make sure to put your full name and the date at the top of your answer page.

Compare and contrast France and the Netherlands in the 17th century. Which culture would you rather have been a part of, and why? Why would you not want to be a part of the other? What would be difficult about living in the county you chose? What would you be giving up by not being a part of the other? Use textual evidence to support your argument. Make sure to use evidence from ALL aspects of the culture (social class, government, economy, and [advanced] religion).

68

Name _____

Class _____

Date _____

Teacher's Section!!

Completeness _____

Comprehension _____

Clarity/Legibility _____

Total Score: _____

Discussion Questions Chapters 14-16

Student Instructions: On the back of this page or a separate sheet of answer the following questions. Be prepared to discuss them with the class. Make sure to put your full name and the date at the top of your answer page.

1. How does the author reestablish the setting (time, place, and background context) in these three chapters? What details does she focus on? What are the first things Etienne notices about his new change in scenery? What does that say about his personality?

2. How does the author use her knowledge of history to recreate the setting of Amsterdam in the 1700's? Compare and contrast her descriptions of Amsterdam to the historical summary we read at the beginning of this part. What details from the summary did she include? What details did she miss that you would have liked to see in the story? Do you see any differences between her description and the summary (make sure to list any differences you see)? Assess the effectiveness of her recreation.

3. How does the author create suspense and a sense of danger in these chapters? What literary techniques or imagery does she use? Would you describe Etienne as a passive or active character in these three chapters? Explain your answer using evidence from the text.

Name _____

Class _____

Date _____

Teacher's Section!!

Completeness _____

Comprehension _____

Clarity/Legibility _____

Total Score: _____

Discussion Questions Chapters 17-19

Student Instructions: On the back of this page or a separate sheet of answer the following questions. Be prepared to discuss them with the class. Make sure to put your full name and the date at the top of your answer page.

1. How does Etienne react when he finds his father? How does this new plot point with his father add/contribute to the plot and/or Etienne's development as a character? Why do you think the author choose to this plot point?

2. In these two chapters, Etienne has to take responsibility for his family and make a lot of hard decisions. What choices does he make for himself and the family? Are these the right decisions? Why or why not? Why did he think they were the right choices or even the only choices he could make? Were there any warning signs and how did he react to them?

3. Create a cause and effect timeline for chapters 14-18 to map out the actions that the characters make, and the effects their actions have on the story and the other characters around them. How do the characters react to an effect? Use different colors, symbols, or positions on the map to show which is the cause (action/event) and which is the effect (result).

Thrown to the Wind Teacher's Resource   *Windy Sea Publishing, LLC*   www.windyseapublishing.com

Name _____

Class _____

Date _____

Teacher's Section!!

Completeness _____

Comprehension _____

Clarity/Legibility _____

Total Score: _____

Discussion Questions Chapters 20-21

Student Instructions: On the back of this page or a separate sheet of answer the following questions. Be prepared to discuss them with the class. Make sure to put your full name and the date at the top of your answer page.

1. In what way and why has Etienne changed since the beginning of the book? Are these good changes or bad changes? Explain your answer using evidence from the text to support your answer.

2. How have Etienne's relationships with the new characters in the story developed? What is his relationship with Po like? How does Chloe react to Etienne's new relationship with Po? What is his relationship like with Magdalena? What does Janssen think about his new relationship with Magdalena? What do the parent's reactions to Etienne's new friendships say about Etienne's social status in this new society? How does this compare with the way François and his friends have treated Etienne his whole life? Use evidence from the text and the historical summary to support your answer.

3. Continue your cause and effect timeline from the last section for chapters 20-21.

Name _____

Class _____

Date _____

Teacher's Section!!

Completeness _____

Comprehension _____

Clarity/Legibility _____

Total Score: _____

Discussion Questions Chapter 22

Student Instructions: On the back of this page or a separate sheet of answer the following questions. Be prepared to discuss them with the class. Make sure to put your full name and the date at the top of your answer page.

1. Continue your cause and effect timeline for chapter 22.

2. Review your cause and effect timeline and use it as evidence for the following questions. Use evidence from the text to answer both questions.

    a. Who or what led Etienne into this position? Whose fault is it that he is stuck on this ship?

    b. Who does Etienne blame for his current situation? Is his anger at this person(s) justified or not? Why or why not?

3. What promise does he make and to whom does he make it? What is the significance of this promise? Where do you think it will lead him?

Name _____

Class _____

Date _____ - _____

Teacher's Section!!

Completeness _____

Comprehension _____

Clarity/Legibility _____

Total Score: _____

Discussion Questions Chapters 23-24

Student Instructions: On the back of this page or a separate sheet of answer the following questions. Be prepared to discuss them with the class. Make sure to put your full name and the date at the top of your answer page.

1. Why did the author title this chapter Baptism? What scene/conversation is she alluding to? What does Etienne's "baptism" symbolize in this chapter? What happened just before this scene in the previous chapter that might add even more significance to this scene. Use evidence from the text to explain and support your answer.

2. After Etienne makes it back to shore, he is hidden by Chloe and Po. He spends several days up there but eventually decides to sneak down to see his parents. What were the consequences of this decision? What are some of the other consequences his action could have caused? What could have happened to him? What could have happened to those around him (Chloe, Po, his parents and siblings, Lena)?

3. Why did Etienne give Po his bowling pins? Who was he think about when he did this? What did this symbolize for Etienne? Why did Lena give him her hair ribbon? What did this small act symbolize between them? Now that Etienne and his family are back on the run, heading toward the "New World," what do you think will happen to him? Will he accomplish his dream of becoming a sailor or will he follow in his father's footsteps? Will he fulfill the promise he made in chapter 22? Explain your predications using evidence from what has already happened in the text.

Name _____

Class _____

Date _____

Teacher's Section!!

Introduction: _____

Narrative: _____

Organization: _____

Language: _____

Total Score: _____

Essay Prompt
Story Rewrite: Cause and Effect Timeline

Student Instructions: Write an essay answering the following prompt. Be prepared to discuss it with the class. Make sure to put your full name and the date at the top of your answer page.

Using your action and effect timeline, rewrite the story changing AT LEAST one action or effect. How would it change the story if Etienne made a different decision or if things played out differently? Rewrite this scene using Etienne's point of view and make sure the story still flows naturally and believably.

74

Name _____

Class _____

Date _____

Teacher's Section!!

Introduction: _____

Narrative: _____

Organization: _____

Language: _____

Total Score: _____

Persuasive Letter to Patron

Student Instructions: Research the 17th century Atlantic merchant trade. Write a persuasive letter to a prospective patron, asking them to support your trading venture to the New Netherlands. In your letter be sure to address and answer the following questions.

1. Where are you going? What to you hope to take and bring back?

2. What are the benefits of this excursion? How will it benefit your patron specifically?

3. What resources do you need (ship, crew, etc.)? How much will this venture cost?

4. How long with the journey take?

5. What are the dangers to be expected? What precautions will you take to try and mitigate them?

Name _____

Class _____

Date _____

<u>**Teacher's Section!!**</u>

Introduction: _____

Narrative: _____

Organization: _____

Language: _____

Total Score: _____

Adventure Journal

Student Instructions: Research the 17th century North American colonies. Imagine that this is your first time arriving in this land that is geographically very different from what you have seen before now.

Write a short story (in the form of personal journal entries) about your adventures in arriving and exploring this new land, and in contacting and conducting business with the people you meet there.

Be sure to use a lot of sensory details and imagery in order to capture the setting. Include sensory details from ALL FIVE senses in your descriptions.

In your journal be sure to address and answer the following questions.

1. Where are you? What does it look like? What plants and animals do you see? What do you hear and smell?

2. What do the people look like? How do they dress? How do they behave?

3. How will you communicate with the people? Do they speak your language? If not, are there interpreters? What signs might you use to communicate?

4. Where will you go when you arrive? How will you travel? What dangers will you face? How will you overcome them?

Part 3: The Voyage

Objectives:

Interpret visual sources to understand historical context.

Interpret primary and secondary sources.

Compare and contrast primary and secondary sources and analyze the purpose each type of source.

Evaluate the accuracy and usefulness of secondary sources in understanding historical events.

Handouts:

- *Thrown to the Wind*, Image 3
- Historical Background for Part 3 with Discussion Questions OR Annotated Historical Background for Part 3 with Discussion Questions
- Research Project
- Discussion Questions by chapter
- Analytical Essay
- Map Project

Day 1

1. **Bell Ringer:** Students will examine the image in the handout "*Thrown to the Wind*, Image 3" and answer the questions. Follow up with a discussion of students' answers.
2. Handout to each student a copy of the **Historical Background for Part 3** or the **Annotated Historical Background for Part 3** and a copy of the **Discussion Questions** and tell students that as they read, they should note any unfamiliar or important words.
   a. <u>With Annotation Guide</u> – Use the annotation guide to identify unknown or important words.
   b. <u>Without Annotation Guide</u> - Underline all the words that appear to be technical history terms (Scaffolded: Use the highlighted words). Use the context around the word to create a guess definition then look up the word in the dictionary.
3. Introduce the **Navigational Tools Research Project** and break students into small groups.
4. Time permitting, allow students to begin their research.

Day 2

1. Student Groups will research their topics and prepare a short presentation.
2. Remind students to keep their bullet points concise phrases, rather than longer sentences and to include images to enhance their presentation.

Days 3 & 4

1. Students will present their research to the class.
2. Students not presenting should take notes on the project worksheet.

Day 5

2. Optional Video: *Women Pirates! Ann Bonny, Mary Read, and Cheng Chi* available on YouTube at:
   https://www.youtube.com/watch?v=he_OyjMilSc
   a. Either watch as a class or have students watch individually and have them take notes about the famous pirates.
   b. (There is a mention to Cheng Chi's former life as "a prostitute on a floating brothel" - time 4:46-50 and an old sketch picture of exposed breasts at the end – time 6:42-47)
3. Students will write an argumentative essay.

Days 6 - 8

1. As students read each section (one or more chapters) ask them to answer the corresponding **"Discussion Questions."** Students could read the chapters at home or in class. The discussion questions may be given out after the students had completed the reading or ahead of time.
2. Conduct a full class discussion or small group round table discussions of the questions.

Day 9
1. Essay/Story Rewrite.
2. Conduct a class discussion of student responses.

Map Project
1. Tell students to create a character and write a short biography for him/her. This character must be a French Huguenot.
2. Students will then research various viable routes the Huguenots might have taken to escape France.
3. Finally, students will create a map to show the route their character took to escape France.

The Trip from La Rochelle to Texel and Amsterdam
Western Europe in the year 1700 Courtesy of the University of Texas Libraries
The University of Texas Austin

Name _____ Class _____ Date _____

Thrown to the Wind, Image 3

De Vergulde Bever (*The Gilded Beaver*) (1660), by Hendrick Cornelisz Vroom, Rijksmuseum, Amsterdam

Answer the following questions:

1. What technological developments would a ship like this need in order to cross the Atlantic Ocean?

2. Based on the visual elements in the image, what is the purpose of this ship? Explain your answer by referencing specific evidence.

3. What kinds of supplies would be needed to survive a trip across the ocean? Of the supplies you listed, which would be the most important? Why?

Individual/Group Activity (For Teachers)

Research Project Instructions

Teacher Instructions: This is an activity where students will research a and share what they have learned about a nautical invention.

1. Vocabulary Assignment: Tell students to underline all the words that appear to be technical history terms (Scaffolded: Use the highlighted words). Whether or not they are already familiar with the word, notice the context around the word to create a guess definition for the word. After that, look up the word in the dictionary and write the exact, relevant definition(s) below their guess.

2. Students (either individually or groups) choose a nautical invention or have one chosen for them to research. They can use the resource links listed above or find their own credible source. They will then become an expert on this invention being able to answer:

    a. When, who, and how it was discovered?
    b. How it is used and why it worked?
    c. How successful it was and/or what other inventions were inspired by it?

3. Students should present it orally to the class. It is recommended that they create a brief PowerPoint or Google slide show to accompany their presentation. The teacher can either have them all present before the class reads Part 3 or at various chapter/chapter group intervals when the author/narrator mention these technological devices in Part 3.

4. Those students listening should take notes on the other student presentations in the blanks and/or separate sheet of paper in the blanks provided under the Navigational Tools section.

Name _____

Class _____

Date _____

Historical Background for
Thrown to the Wind Part 3:
History of the Ocean Explorations

Nautical Discoveries and Inventions

Ships

      The first boat historians have evidence for is a rowboat in Egypt used for navigating the Nile River. From there, Egyptians began sea voyages to other nearby countries, spreading the technology to other civilizations.[46] Every civilization put their spin on boat design. Egypt and other Mediterranean countries focused on rowing technology. However, in the Baltics, the strong, frequently shifting winds, encouraged the use of some of the first sails.

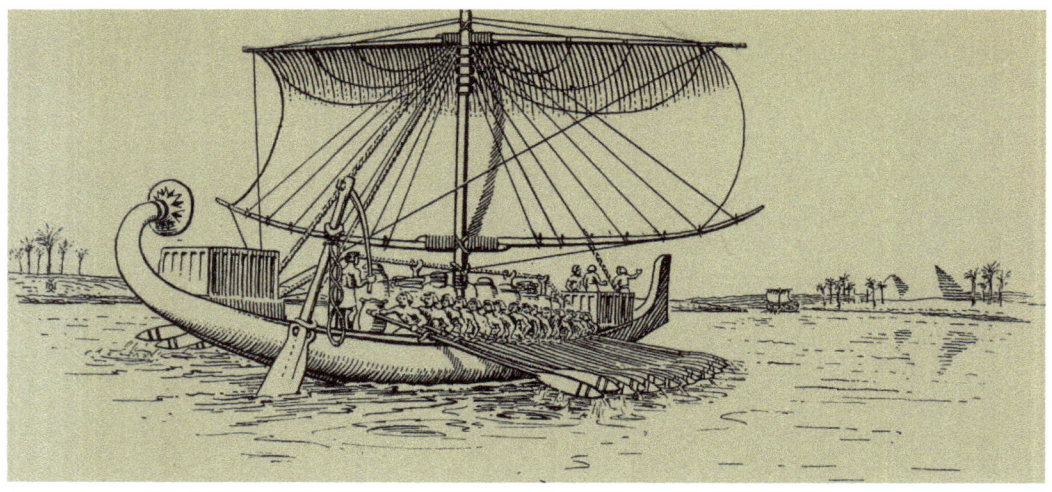

The Romance of the Ship: The Story of Her Origin and Evolution

By E. Keble Chatterton (1878-1944), J.B. Lippincott Company, Philadelphia, 1911. Publish Domain

      However, there was a push to increase sailing technology as it saved human resources and increased efficiency. So, ships started moving away from the single square canvas sail to a complex rigging that could pivot with wind changes allowing vessels to sail "into the wind."[47]

      As ships became more prevalent for world trade, the search for faster and larger vessels led to many innovations in ship technology. To increase propulsion, ship designers started adding more and more sails, which forced them to add more masts to the ship and, ultimately, elongate the ship hulls. These were called "full-rigged" ships.

---

[46] James Joseph Stilwell and James E. Vance, *Ship*, "History of Ships", (Encyclopedia Britanica, inc., June 22, 2018).

[47] James Joseph Stilwell and James E. Vance, *Ship*.

(1) Jib
(2) Fore upper topsail
(3) Fore lower topsail
(4) Foresail
(5) Main upper topsail
(6) Main lower topsail
(7) Mainsail
(8) Mizzen upper topsail
(9) Mizzen lower topsail
(10) Crossjack
(11) Spanker or driver

Spars, sails, and rigging of a full-rigged Galleon ship.
DALL·E 2024-12-19 16.08.38 -A detailed side view of a historical galleon ship without any text labels. The ship features multiple masts with various sails including the mainsail

One of the most successful and popular "full-rigged" ship was the galleon, used from the 16th to 18th centuries. Originating in Spain, shipbuilders designed these ships with longer hulls that allowed them to ride lower in the water, giving them more stability and reducing wind resistance.[48] Because of their advantage in speed and stability, many other countries adopted and adapted them. Galleons were versatile ships that were used for trade but could also be drafted and easily adapted for war. The Dutch East Indies Trading Company particularly loved them as they could carry large amounts of trade goods and still be armed to protect against pirates.[49]

Lateen-rigged ship (right)
DALL·E 2024-12-19 16.37.06 - A detailed side view of a lateen-rigged fishing ship, showcasing its triangular sails mounted on angled yards attached to the masts.

---

[48] Timothy R. Walton, *The Spanish Treasure Fleets,* (Pineapple Press Inc, 2002), p. 57.
[49] Kris E. Lane, *Pillaging the Empire: Piracy in the Americas 1500-1750,* (M. E. Sharpe, 1998).l;`

Name _____ Class _____ Date _____

Navigational Tools Research Element

Directions: *Students will take notes in the blanks on the questions provided during presentations.*

- Mariner's Magnetic Compass
    - Date Invented:

    - Inventor:

    - Why/How it was Invented:

    - How it Works:

    - Additional Information:

- Navigational Charts
    - Date Invented:

    - Inventor:

    - Why/How it was Invented:

    - How it Works:

    - Additional Information:

- Celestial Navigation

- Date Invented:

- Inventor:

- Why/How it was Invented:

- How it Works:

- Additional Information:

Latitudinal Instruments
- Astrolabe
  - Date Invented:
  - Inventor:
  - Why/How it was Invented:

  - How it Works:

  - Additional Information:

- Quadrant
  - Date Invented:
  - Inventor:
  - Why/How it was Invented:

- How it Works:

- Additional Information:

- Cross Staff
  - Date Invented:
  - Inventor:
  - Why/How it was Invented:
  - How it Works:
  - Additional Information:

- Astronomical Charts
  - Date Invented:
  - Inventor:
  - Why/How it was Invented:
  - How it Works:
  - Additional Information:

Depth/Speed Instruments
- Sandglass/hourglass
  - Date Invented:
  - Inventor:
  - Why/How it was Invented:
  - How it Works:
  - Additional Information:

- Chip Log
  - Date Invented:
  - Inventor:
  - Why/How it was Invented:
  - How it Works:
  - Additional Information:

- Leadline
  - Date Invented:
  - Inventor:
  - Why/How it was Invented:

- How it Works:

- Additional Information:

Other Instruments
- Ship's Log
  - Date Invented:
  - Inventor:
  - Why/How it was Invented:
  - How it Works:
  - Additional Information:

Helpful Links to Help Research
1. "History of Navigation at Sea: From Starts to Modern Day GPS," *Formula*. https://www.formulaboats.com/blog/history-of-navigation-at-sea/
2. "8 Tools We Used to Navigate the World Around Us Before GPS and Smartphones." *CityLab*. https://www.citylab.com/life/2013/04/7-examples-how-we-used-navigate-world-around-us/5286/
3. "Time and Navigation," *Smithsonian*. https://timeandnavigation.si.edu/timeline2
4. "History of Navigation," *Preceden*. https://www.preceden.com/timelines/316316-history-of-navigation
5. "Navigation and Related Instruments int the 16th Century England," *Fort Raleigh National Historic Site*. https://www.nps.gov/fora/learn/education/navigation-and-related-instruments-in-16th-century-england.htm
6. "10 Top Innovations in the History of Sailing," *Yachting and Boating World*. https://www.ybw.com/features/10-top-innovations-in-the-history-of-sailing-17358

Age of Exploration Timeline – The Americas[50]

Pre-Columbus

- Some theorists believe that about 13,000 BCE hunters and fishers from Asia (whom archeologists called Pre-Clovis) discovered the Americas and spent approximately 12,000 years exploring the coastlines and colonizing.
- **970 CE:** Viking Explorer Erik the Red discovered Greenland and began a colony there.
- **998 CE:** Erik the Red's son Leif Erikson reached Newfoundland and explored the region.
- **1473 CE:** Portuguese sailor Joao Vaz Corte-Real explored the coast of North America and called it Terra Nova do Bacalhau (New Land of Codfish)

Columbus and Later Explorations

- **1492-1493 CE:** Italian Explorer Christopher Columbus made three voyages (paid for by the Spanish government) trying to prove that he could circumnavigate around the globe and reach the West Indies. Instead, he landed on islands off the coast of North America. However, he believed he had successfully landed in the West Indies and therefore named the inhabitants "Indians."
- **1500 CE:** Italian Explorer and cartographer Amerigo Vespucci explored the Brazilian coast and realized (unlike Columbus) that he had found a new continent. The continent was later named America after him, against his wishes.
- **1513 CE:** The mad dash to claim new territory began. European countries started funding explorers to travel to the "New World" in order to claim new land for their governments.

Permanent European Settlements

- **1565:** Spanish admiral and explorer Pedro Menendez de Aviles founded settled the first permanent European settlement at St. Augustine, Florida (discovered in 1513 by Spanish Explorer Juan Ponce de León).

- **1584:** English writer, poet, soldier, politician, courtier, spy, and explorer Walter Raleigh (1552–1618) landed on Roanoke Island and called the land Virginia in honor of Queen Elizabeth.

- **1585:** Colonists settled in Roanoke in Virginia. However, this was a short-lived colony. Shortly after the colony was established, the Roanoke governor, John White, journeyed back to England. When he returned two years later, the colony had disappeared with little evidence left behind. England attempted to recolonize Roanoke, but after White left for the second time and when he returned in 1590, the settlement had yet again disappeared. To this day, mystery surrounds their disappearance.

[Added content from here down.]

- **1607:** Jamestown was established in Virginia under a charter to the London Company as a money-making venture. Early settlers came in search of mineral riches but did not find any. The colony nearly failed until John Rolfe obtained tobacco plants from the Spanish and brought them to Jamestown. Tobacco turned out to be a very profitable industry that led to the development of large plantations requiring first indentured servants and eventually slaves to plant, harvest, and process the tobacco leaves for shipment back to England.

---

[50] Copied directly from Martin Kelly, *A Timeline of North American Exploration, 1492-1585,* (ThoughtCo) Feb. 11, 2020.

- **1620:** Pilgrims, Calvinist Separatists, who wanted to separate from the Church of England, obtained a charter from King James I of England to establish a community in the northern region of Virginia. The ships landed too far north, but decided to stay, establishing the Plymouth Colony. The Pilgrim's laid the foundation for self-government in the English colonies by signing the *Mayflower* Compact upon arrival, agreeing to select their leaders and to be bound by the laws established. This colony would eventually be combined with the Massachusetts Bay Colony in 1691.

- **1625:** New Netherlands was founded by the Dutch, extending from Manhattan Island up the Hudson River. This colony was established to facilitate the fur trade with the Native Americans, though not all of their dealings with the natives were peaceful. From the beginning, this was a diverse colony represented by people of numerous nationalities, languages, and religions. In 1664, the British would conquer this colony and rename it New York.

- **1629:** Massachusetts Bay Colony was a joint-stock venture in which Puritans, Calvinist Protestants wanting to "purify" the Anglican Church of "Popish" or Catholic influences, obtained a charter from King Charles I to establish the colony. This was the first English company for which their governing board were located in the colony and not back in England. This colony also began to establish the precedence of self-government in the colonies, though men had to be members of the Congregational Church in order to vote or participate in politics.

The Golden Age of Piracy: 1650-1725

With the invention of better ships (such as the galleons) and navigational tools, and with the discovery of the New World and its bountiful resources, world trade and conquest became a dominate way for European countries to stay ahead. However, with such active shipping lanes and inactive government regulations or protection, this also opened a large door to piracy. There was no lack of volunteers to crew these pirate ships, as many European farmers were being pushed off their land by larger corporate farms or factories. Many workers were driven to work in the new factories that refined the goods being shipped in from the New World. However, many others turned to the sea for work, signing onto trade ships and later being impressed onto the highly profitable pirate ships. As slavery developed in the American colonies, many fleeing the institution found work on merchant and pirate ships, where questions were seldom asked.

Jean-David Nau, L'Olonnais was a French buccaneer, which is a cross between a privateer commissioned by the government and an outlaw pirate. He was nicknamed François L'Olonnais, and "Flail of the Spaniards."[51] He roamed the Caribbean Sea in the mid to late 1660s and is believed to have started raiding Spanish ships and coastal settlements.[52] He quickly earned a reputation for using excessive cruelty. He first arrived in the Caribbean in 1650, when he was fifteen years old, and worked for ten years as an indentured servant,[53] or someone who has paid for the fare with the promise to work off the debt. In 1660 he joined the buccaneers robbing and killing Spaniards.[54] "Seventeenth-century pirate historian Alexander Exquemelin wrote that L'Olonnais would hack his victims to pieces bit by bit or squeeze a cord around their necks until their eyes popped out."[55] Once when L'Olonnais suspected that he had been betrayed, he supposedly cut the man's heart out and took a bite of it.[56] According to Exquemelin, in 1668, he received his just due when he was captured and eaten by cannibals.[57]

---

[51] *The Way of the Pirates,* "Famous Buccaneer: Francois L'Ollonais," (2020).
[52] Jesse Greenspan, *The History Channel,* "8 Real-Life Pirates Who Roved the High Seas," (Aug.31, 2018).
[53] *The Way of Pirates*
[54] ibn
[55] Jesse Greenspan, *The History Channel.*
[56] ibn
[57] ibn

Name _____ Class _____ Date _____

Fun Fact: Women Pirates! Anne Bonny, Mary Read, and Cheng Chi
Video Time! IT'S HISTORY: The Most Famous Female PIRATES of All Time! (7:41 min.)
https://www.youtube.com/watch?v=he_OyjMiISc

As you watch, answer the questions below.
1. List three facts about Anne Bonny.

    a. _____

    b. _____

    c. _____

2. List three facts about Mary Read.

    a. _____

    b. _____

    c. _____

3. Why were Anne and Mary eventually caught? How were they able to escape the hangman's noose?

    _____
    _____
    _____
    _____
    _____

4. How did Ching Shih build a piracy empire? How many ships and pirates did she control?

    _____
    _____
    _____
    _____
    _____

5. List two of Ching Shih's rules for her pirates?

   a. _____

   b. _____

6. What deal did the Chen Emperor make with Ching Shih?

7. Do you think the stories of women pirates are a story of liberation for women, or not? Explain your answer.

Name _____

Class _____

Date _____

Teacher's Section!!
Completeness _____
Comprehension _____
Clarity/Legibility _____
Total Score: _____

Discussion Questions Chapters 25-27

Student Instructions: On the back of this page or a separate sheet of answer the following questions. Be prepared to discuss them with the class. Make sure to put your full name and the date at the top of your answer page.

1. Throughout the novel, François has been antagonizing Etienne. Why do you think he does this? What is his motivation in tormenting Etienne? What is François' father like? Was Etienne justified in his violent reaction? Why or why not? What other reactions could Etienne have had? Yet, despite the animosity between the two characters, Etienne didn't even hesitate to save François in the storm scene. What does this say about Etienne's character? Why didn't François show more gratitude to Etienne? What does this say about his personality? Use textual evidence to support your answers.

2. In these chapters, Etienne meets Jan, the cabin boy of the *Gilded Beaver*. How would you describe this new character? What adjectives would you use? These characters are very close in age, how does he compare to Etienne? In what ways does Jan represent what Etienne could have become? Support your answer using textual evidence.

3. Throughout these three chapters, Etienne is repeatedly reminded of the biblical story of Jonah and the Whale. According to Christian mythology, Jonah was ordered by the Christian God to preach to a foreign country known for being violent. Instead, however, Jonah was afraid to go, so he got on a boat heading in the opposite direction. As the myth goes, God sent a terrible storm to plaque the ship Jonah was on. The sailors were afraid and blamed Jonah for setting the storm upon them. So, Jonah, knowing there was no other way, instructed the sailors to throw him overboard. The storm stopped, and God sent a large fish to swallow Jonah whole. After three days and nights living in the stomach of the creature, the fish spit him onto the shore of the country he was originally supposed to go to.

    Why did Etienne think of this story in this situation? How is his story similar? How is his story different? Why did the author choose the use this allusion in this place. Based on what happened in the previous part as well as what's happening in these three chapters, what does this allegory symbolize or represent? How does it add or contribute to the plot? Use textual evidence to support your answer.

Thrown to the Wind Teacher's Resource *Windy Sea Publishing, LLC* www.windyseapublishing.com

Name _____

Class _____

Date _____

Teacher's Section!!

Completeness _____

Comprehension _____

Clarity/Legibility _____

Total Score: _____

Discussion Questions Chapters 28-30

Student Instructions: On the back of this page or a separate sheet of answer the following questions. Be prepared to discuss them with the class. Make sure to put your full name and the date at the top of your answer page.

1. In the chapter, "Trouble at Sea," Etienne again saves another Lefevre brother, this time Tomas. What are the reactions of both brothers? How does Tomas react? How does François react? Why are their reactions so different? What insight does Tomas reveal about François? Does this change your opinion of François? Why or why not?

2. How has Etienne grown or changed throughout the novel? What did he used to be like? What is he like now? Are these changes for the better? Looking back over the events that happened to him and his reactions to these scenarios, what caused such a transformation in Etienne's character?

3. At the end of Part 3, Lidie gets very sick with scurvy and Etienne tells her she needs to be strong and hold on. What does she say in return that shocks and surprises him? What reaction does this have on Etienne? Do you think she actually saw Louis? Why would the author bring in this element into the story? What effects might this have later on in the story for Etienne?

Name _____

Class _____

Date _____

Teacher's Section!!
Claim: _____
Evidence: _____
Organization: _____
Language: _____
Total Score: _____

Essay Prompt
Character Analysis: Etienne's Development

Student Instructions: Write an essay answering the following prompt. Be prepared to discuss it with the class. Make sure to put your full name and the date at the top of your answer page.

How has Etienne grown or developed as a character? What changes have you seen in him since the beginning of the novel? Are these good or bad changes? Explain your position. Use evidence from the text to support your answer.

94

Individual/Group Project
Map Project

Teacher's Section!!

Research: _____

Character Analysis:

_____

Organization: _____

Language: _____

Preparation/Presentation:

_____

Total Score: _____

Student Instructions: As individuals or in groups, follow the instructions below to create your own constellation and accompanying myth.

1. Create a character and write a short bio for him/her. This character must be a French Huguenot.

2. Answer the following questions about your character in the bio.

    a. What is his/her name?

    b. What is his/her profession?

    c. What was his/her childhood like?

    d. Was (s)he raised protestant or raised Catholic? If he/she was raised Catholic when and why did the character convert?

    e. Is (s)he married? If so, do they have kids? What other family members does (s)he have?

3. Research the various routes Huguenots took to escape France. Answer the following questions.

    a. List the different routes out of France as well as the various destinations.

    b. How much distance is there between France and the final destinations?

    c. What were the dangers of each route?

    d. What major landmarks and geographic terrains (AKA mountains, forests, rivers, lakes, etc.) would they have passed through?

    e. What is the cost of this route approximately? Various payment options.

    f. Is your character travelling with family? If so, who and how will that factor into your escape route?

4. Create a map

    a. Make sure to include a key/legend of landmarks and geographic stuff.

    b. Add lines that mark the journey as well as 3D images of the type of transport used.

    c. Make sure to include the scale and keep it accurate. Use a ruler.

    d. Include a compass rose.

Part 4: A New World

Objectives:

Interpret visual sources to understand historical context.

Interpret primary and secondary sources.

Compare and contrast primary and secondary sources and analyze the purpose each type of source.

Evaluate the accuracy and usefulness of secondary sources in understanding historical events.

Handouts:
- *Thrown to the Wind*, Image 4
- Historical Background for Part 4 with Discussion Questions
- Discussion Questions by chapter
- Essay Idea List
- Wrap-up Project List

Day 1
1. **Bell Ringer:** Students will examine the image in the handout "*Thrown to the Wind*, Image 4" and answer the questions. Follow up with a discussion of students' answers.
2. Handout to each student a copy of the **Historical Background for Part 4** with a copy of the **Discussion Questions** and tell students that as they read, they should note any unfamiliar or important words.
    a. <u>Annotation Guide</u> – Not provided with this unit.
    b. <u>Without Annotation Guide</u> - Underline all the words that appear to be technical history terms <u>(Scaffolded</u>: Use the highlighted words). Use the context around the word to create a guess definition then look up the word in the dictionary.

Day 2
1. As students read the section (one or more chapters) ask them to answer the corresponding **"Discussion Questions."** Students could read the chapters at home or in class. The discussion questions may be given out after the students had completed the reading or ahead of time.
2. Conduct a full class discussion or small group round table discussions of the questions.

Day(s) 3 – 5
1. Essay prompt: Teacher may choose one of the essay prompts provided or may choose of offer students a choice.
2. Teacher may choose to give a one-day essay prompt as a formal assessment or the teacher may opt to allow more than one day for the essay, in order that students may revise and edit their essays before final submission.

Wrap-up Project List
1. Extension Activity: Several ideas are provided as extension ideas in addition to, or in place of the above essay prompt, to provide students an opportunity to demonstrate their knowledge of this unit.

96

Name _____ Class _____ Date _____

Thrown to the Wind, Image 4

A view of New Amsterdam from Governor's Island
Manhattan 1660, by Len Tantillo

Answer the following questions:

1. On the left end of the island, there is a large windmill. What purpose did windmills serve?

2. A stone wall encloses a portion of the city of New Amsterdam. The flag and several buildings are visible behind the wall. What purpose did the wall serve? What purposes would the buildings in this enclosure serve?

3. What else can you infer about this city, based on the visual elements depicted? Explain your answer.

Name _____

Class _____

Date _____

Historical Background for
Thrown to the Wind Part 4:
History of New Amsterdam

New Amsterdam

In the year 1624, The Dutch West India Trading Company (WIC) established the colony of New Amsterdam on what is now called Manhattan Island in New York City, New York.[58] The Italian explorer Giovanni de Verrazzano initially discovered the territory in the year 1524.[59] The first Dutch exploration of the area was in 1609, under the leadership of English explorer, Henry Hudson, and, upon his return to the Netherlands, he reported back about the abundance of beaver in the area.[60] Beaver pelts, as well as other types of fur, were popular in Europe because they were used to make water-resistant hats and castoreum, a bitter strong-smelling creamy orange-brown substance that came from the perineal glands of the beaver, which was known to have certain medicinal properties and was also used to make perfume.[61] After several other exploration attempts, the Dutch finally settled the area, naming their new territory, The New Netherlands, and establishing colony cities such as Fort Orange and New Amsterdam.

New Amsterdam, situated at the mouth the Hudson River (what the Dutch called the *Noort Rivier*, or North River), gave the settlers easy access to the ocean as well as to the beaver trading posts upriver.

Initially, the settlers' interactions with Native Americans were pretty rocky due to the brutal policies Director Willem Kieft established in 1637. These policies led to a war that threatened the colony's existence.[62] However, the natives and settlers managed to establish peace in 1645. For many years, there was a tentative peace between the settlers and colonists. Native American hunters would trade belts with the settlers in exchange for European-made goods such as cooking pots, guns, and tools. However, in 1655, New Amsterdam was attacked by 600 Native Americans in the Peach Tree War. There were many casualties, including the destruction of twenty-eight farms, a hundred dead settlers, and another hundred fifty settlers taken as prisoners.[63] There continued to be several raids and retaliation that came from both sides; however, these tended to be short-lived, and trade ruled in most of the relations between the natives and settlers.

---

[58] *This Day in History,* "New Amsterdam becomes New York," (The History Channel, July 27, 2019) Accessed May 19, 2020.
[59] Biography.com Editors, *Biography,* "Giovannie da Verrazzano," (A&E Televison Networks, August 22, 2019) Accessed May 19, 2020.
[60] "The Story of New Amsterdam," (New Amsterdam History Center, 2011).
[61] *Merriam-Webster Dictionary,* "Castoreum," (Merriam-Webster, Accessed May 19, 2020).
[62] "Willem Kieft (1597-1647)," (New Netherlands Institute).
[63] *Wikipedia,* "Peach Tree War," (March 21, 2020).

98

Name _____

Class _____

Date _____

Teacher's Section!!

Completeness _____

Comprehension _____

Clarity/Legibility _____

Total Score: _____

Discussion Questions

Student Instructions: On the back of this page or a separate sheet of answer the following questions. Be prepared to discuss them with the class. Make sure to put your full name and the date at the top of your answer page.

Vocabulary Assignment: Underline all the words that appear to be technical history terms (Scaffolded: Use the highlighted words). Whether or not you are already familiar with the word, se the context around the word to create a guess definition for the word. After that, look up the word in the dictionary and write the exact, relevant definition(s) below your guess.

1. What is the central idea/topic of this text? Use textual evidence to support your answer.

2. What is the purpose of the text? Use textual evidence to support your answer.

3. Does the author show any bias? If so to what/whom? Use textual evidence to support your answer.

Name _____

Class _____

Date _____

Teacher's Section!

Claim:

_____

Evidence: _____

Organization: _____

Language: _____

Discussion Questions Chapters 31-Epilogue

Student Instructions: On the back of this page or a separate sheet of answer the following questions. Be prepared to discuss them with the class. Make sure to put your full name and the date at the top of your answer page.

1. New Amsterdam is the last new setting the author establishes. How does her description compare and contrast with the pictures and paintings you looked at before reading through this part?

2. Would you describe Etienne in this part as an active or passive character? What decisions does he make? Who does he disobey? Do you think he makes the right decisions? Why or why not?

3. Did the other characters in this chapter think Etienne made the right decisions? Why did Jan help him? What does this say about his views on Etienne's actions? How did Etienne's father react when he returned to the ship and how does that let us know what his father's thinks of his actions? Why did Etienne's mom step in between Etienne and his father when he returned? What does this say about what she thinks of Etienne's actions? Support you answer using textual evidence.

4. In the chapter "Cherries," Etienne sees a familiar face, whose face did he see? What is the significance of seeing her in New Amsterdam? What might this mean for the story. Lidie also sees someone familiar. Who was it, and what message did that someone leave for Etienne? What is the significance of this encounter for the story? Explain you answer using textual evidence.

Thrown to the Wind Teacher's Resource   *Windy Sea Publishing, LLC*   www.windyseapublishing.com

5. At the end of the chapter "Cherries," Etienne meets a Native America girl named Alsoome. What does she claim her name means? While her presence in the book is short, do you think she has lived up to her name meaning? What does it say about her personality that she is the only person to help Etienne? Did she ask for anything in return and if so what and why is that an important observation to make about her?

6. The last chapter in the book is titled, "Forgiveness." Why do you think the author chose this title? Who does it apply to?

7. Why do you think the author chose to write the epilogue? What value did it bring to the story? Explain your answer using textual evidence.

Essay Prompt
Wrap-up Essay Ideas

Student Instructions: Choose one of the following essay prompts, and write an essay answering your chosen prompt. Be prepared to discuss it with the class. Make sure to put your full name and the date at the top of your answer page.

1. How did Etienne's mother change throughout the story? While she appears to be a small character, why is she so important to the story? In what ways did she help drive the story forward?

2. Trace and evaluate Etienne and François' relationship. Why was this relationship so important to the story? How does it reflect Etienne's character growth?

3. Is disobedience for a good cause justified? Why or why not? How would Etienne answer this question? How might Etienne's father answer it? His mother? How would the author answer it?

4. How might Etienne's story connect to current immigration stories today? Is there a connection? What are some similarities? What are some differences? What lessons about immigration can we learn from Etienne?

5. Why was there so much animosity between the Protestants and Catholics? How does the religious persecution in the book and in history relate to us today? Do we see the same issues in our society? What does this say about humanity? What should be our response to differing belief systems?

102

Name _____

Class _____

Date _____

Wrap-Up Book Projects

> **Teacher's Section!**
>
> Preparation & Collaboration: _____
>
> Content & Completion: _____
>
> Presentation & Articulation: _____
>
> Total Score: _____

Student Instructions: As a group, choose one of the following project ideas and work together to create the project, answer the questions, and create a presentation.

1. Movie Poster

    Materials:
    - Poster board
    - Crayons, markers, and/or colored pencils

    Instructions:
    - On one side of the poster, create a graphic image that will appeal to an audience and make them want to see the movie adaptation. Create and include a cast list for the characters using famous or popular actors.
    - On the other side, answer the following questions:
        a. What is your poster showing?
        b. Why did you choose/create/design this image?
        c. Explain your casting decisions. Why did you choose each actor? What other movies was the actor in? What character traits were you looking for in each actor? What character traits (physical or personality) are you giving up by casting this particular actor?

2. Movie or Documentary Trailer

    Materials:
    - Paper
    - Crayons, markers, and/or colored pencils

    Instructions:
    - Create a story board for a trailer either for a movie adaptation of the book or for a documentary about the Huguenots. Choose and include at least 6 scenes from the book. For each scene create a:
        a. Graphic image of the scene
        b. An explanation of what the scene is showing
        c. An explanation of why you chose to include this scene in your trailer.

3. Diorama

    Materials:
    - Box (shoe, cardboard, tissue)
    - Something to make figurines and set pieces
        - Modeling clay
        - Popsicle sticks and paper
        - Legos
        - Etc.

    Instructions:
    - Create a 3-Dimensional replica of an important scene from the novel.

- On a separate sheet of paper answer the following questions:
    a. What scene did you choose? Provide a paragraph summary of the scene you chose to display.
    b. What stage in the novel is this in?
        o Exposition
        o Inciting Incident
        o Rising Action
        o Climax
        o Resolution
    c. Why did you choose this scene? Why do you consider this scene important to the novel?

4. Persuasive Letter

    Materials:
    - Paper and Pen or Computer/Laptop

    Instructions:
    - Imagine that a school is considering adding this book to their English Language Arts curriculum. Write a persuasive letter to the school board explaining why you would or would not recommend this book for their curriculum.
    - The essay should be AT LEAST five paragraphs including an introductory paragraph and a concluding paragraph.
    - Make sure to plan out your argument, listing reasons you would recommend it and reasons you would not recommend it. You should include both even if your argument is for one or the other. You will include this organizer with the essay.
    - Make sure to textual evidence to support your argument.

5. Interview a Character

    Materials:
    - Costumes and Props for characters
    - Set pieces (chairs, tables, tablecloths, etc.)

    Instructions:
    - Your group will be acting out a character interview. One person in the group will be the interviewer and the others will each play the role of a character.
    - Create a script of questions (for the interviewer) and answers (for the characters). This script should include at least 5 questions for each character being interviewed. These questions should require more than one-word answers.
    - With your script, you should also include a short explanation of why you chose to interview each character.
    - As you act out the interview, make sure either to memorize your lines or that everyone has their own copy of the script and to try to speak and act like the character you are portraying.

Appendix A
Checklists and Rubrics

1. Checklist for Evaluating Sources
2. Discussion Question Rubric
3. Discussion Question and Annotation Rubric
4. Argumentative Essay Rubric
5. Informative Essay Rubric
6. Narrative Essay Rubric
7. Presentation Rubric
8. Research Project Rubric

Name: _____   Class: _____   Date: _____

Checklist for Evaluating Sources

Use the following checklist to evaluate the reliability of the source material:

Author, Editor, or Creator:

_____   Did a reliable person or organization create this document?

_____   Is the author, editor, or creator an expert on the topic?

_____   Can you confirm the credentials of the source?

Content:

_____   Is the information based on fact or opinion?

_____   Is the content balanced, addressing multiple points of view, or one-sided?
(If the source has a particular bias, be sure to balance it out with sources of opposing perspectives.)

_____   Is the information complete and accurate, compared to other sources read?

_____   What is the point of view of the source? How objective is it?
(Check for use of emotional words, exaggerations, direct promotion of a specific view.)

Context:

_____   What is the purpose of the document? Is it meant to educate or persuade?

_____   How have the major events or beliefs from the time the source was written or produced influenced this document?

_____   Does the information cite other reliable sources?

Name: _____ Class: _____ Date: _____

Discussion Question Rubric

Weight	Category	Incomplete 1	Minimally Proficient 2	Partially Proficient 3	Proficient 4	Highly Proficient 5
x1	Completeness Standards: 7.RI/RL.10; 7.L.6	Student has failed to answer many of the questions, has missed most parts of the questions, and/or has written one word or one sentence responses.	Student has answered some of the questions but not all or student has missed parts of some of the questions. Student has missed several key elements or themes in their answers. Student might have only written a sentence or two for each paragraph.	Student has answered all parts of all the questions, but answers do not fully explore the topic. Student might have missed a key element or theme in their answer. Student has written at least a short paragraph for each response.	All responses are thorough and answer all parts of all the questions. Student has written at least a complete paragraph for each response.	All responses are thorough and answer all parts of all the questions, even going above and beyond, adding insight not directly asked for. Student has written more than a complete paragraph for each response.
x3	Comprehension Standards: 7.RI/RL.1-3, 5, 6, 9	Student displays minimal or no understanding of the topic/central idea, text structure, author point of view and/or literary/technical elements of the text. Student does not use evidence to support their explanation.	Student displays some understanding of the topic/central idea, text structure, author point of view and/or literary/technical elements of the text. Student uses evidence, but it may be confusing or disconnected from their analysis.	Student displays a basic understanding of the topic/central idea, text structure, author point of view and/or literary/technical elements of the text. Student uses evidence, but it may not be the strongest example and/or may not clearly connect to their analysis.	All responses display a complete understanding of the topic/central idea, text structure, author point of view and/or literary/technical elements of the text. Student uses relevant evidence and connects it to their analysis.	All responses display a complete, complex and insightful understanding of the topic/central idea, text structure, author point of view, and/or literary/technical elements of the text. Student chooses strong and relevant evidence and clearly connects it to their analysis.
x1	Clarity/Legibility Standards: 7.RI/RL.4; 7.L.1-5	Student's text is barely legible due to many grammar and spelling mistakes.	Student has several grammar or spelling mistakes.	Student uses correct grammar and spelling.	Student uses correct grammar and spelling, choosing appropriate, interesting language (including any technical terminology from the text) to add variety to the text.	Student uses correct grammar and spelling. Student chooses appropriate, interesting language (including any technical terminology from the text) and factors in connotation and context in order to add variety, precision, and conciseness to the text.

Teacher Comments:

Name: _____ Class: _____ Date: _____

Discussion Question and Annotation Rubric

Weight	Category	Incomplete 1	Minimally Proficient 2	Partially Proficient 3	Proficient 4	Highly Proficient 5
x1	Completeness Standards: 7.RI.10; 7.L.6	Student has failed to answer many of the questions, has missed most parts of the questions, and/or has written one word or one sentence responses. Student has not put any effort into completing their annotation guide.	Student has answered some of the questions but not all or student has missed parts of some of the questions. Student has missed several key elements or themes in their answers. Student might have only written a sentence or two for each paragraph. Student is missing many elements in their annotation guide.	Student has answered all parts of all the questions, but answers do not fully explore the topic. Student might have missed a key element or theme in their answer. Student has written at least a short paragraph for each response. Student is some key elements in their annotation guide.	All responses are thorough and answer all parts of all the questions. Student has written at least a complete paragraph for each response. Student has completed all parts of their annotations guide.	All responses are thorough and answer all parts of all the questions, even going above and beyond, adding insight not directly asked for. Student has written more than a complete paragraph for each response. Student has completed all parts of annotation guide and provided additional insight in their comments and answers.
x3	Comprehension Standards: 7.RI.1-3, 5, 6	Student displays minimal or no understanding of the topic/central idea, text structure, author point of view and/or literary/technical elements of the text. Student does not use evidence to support their explanation.	Student displays some understanding of the topic/central idea, text structure, author point of view and/or literary/technical elements of the text. Student uses evidence, but it may be confusing or disconnected from their analysis.	Student displays a basic understanding of the topic/central idea, text structure, author point of view and/or literary/technical elements of the text. Student uses evidence, but it may not be the strongest example and/or may not clearly connect to their analysis.	All responses display a complete understanding of the topic/central idea, text structure, author point of view and/or literary/technical elements of the text. Student uses relevant evidence and connects it to their analysis.	All responses display a complete, complex, and insightful understanding of the topic/central idea, text structure, author point of view, and/or literary/technical elements of the text. Student chooses clear, strong, and relevant evidence and clearly connects it to their analysis.
x1	Clarity/Legibility Standards: 7.RI.4; 7.L.1-5	Student's text is barely legible due to many grammar and spelling mistakes.	Student has several grammar or spelling mistakes.	Student uses correct grammar and spelling.	Student uses correct grammar and spelling, choosing appropriate, interesting language (including any technical terminology from the text) to add variety to the text.	Student uses correct grammar & spelling. Student chooses appropriate, interesting language (including any technical terminology from the text) and factors in connotation and context in order to add variety, precision, and conciseness to the text.

Teacher Comments:

Name: _____ Class: _____ Date: _____

Argumentative Essay Rubric

Weight	Category	Incomplete 1	Minimally Proficient 2	Partially Proficient 3	Proficient 4	Highly Proficient 5
x1	Claim Standards: 7.W.1a, 4	The student does not have a clear or arguable claim.	Student makes a claim, but it may be hard to identify and/or not in the introduction. Student does not acknowledge alternate or opposing claims. Few points, arguments, or evidence points back to the claim.	Student makes an arguable claim in the introduction. Student tries to acknowledge alternate or opposing claims but may not do so accurately or fairly. Throughout the essay, most points, arguments, and evidence point back to the claim.	Student makes an arguable claim in the introduction. Student also acknowledges and refutes alternate or opposing claims. Throughout the essay, all points, arguments, and evidence point back to the claim.	Student makes a clear, solid, and arguable claim in the introduction. Student also acknowledges and effectively refutes alternate or opposing claims. Throughout the essay, all points, arguments, and evidence clearly point back to the claim.
x2	Evidence Standards: 7.W.1b, 4	Claims presented are not supported with evidence.	Not all claims presented are supported with evidence. Evidence comes from sources that may or may not be credible or accurate and/or may not be correctly cited.	All claims presented are supported with evidence or logical reasoning. Evidence comes from accurate and credible sources but may not be correctly cited.	All claims presented are supported with relevant evidence and logical reasoning. Evidence comes from accurate and credible sources and is correctly cited.	All claims presented are supported with clear, strong, and relevant evidence and insightful, logical reasoning. Evidence comes from accurate, credible, and interesting sources written by experts and is correctly cited.
x1	Organization Standards: 7.W.1c, 1e, 4	The essay has no clear structure or transitions between ideas.	Student includes an introduction, body, and conclusion in the essay but doesn't write complete paragraphs or sentences. The introduction may not include a claim while the conclusion may only consist of a generalities or filler sentences.	Student includes an introduction, body, and conclusion in the essay. The introduction includes a claim while the conclusion attempts to wrap up the argument by simply rephrasing or repeating the claim. Student attempts to use transition words, phrases, or clauses but essay might still feel choppy.	Student includes a clear introduction, body, and conclusion in the essay. The introduction includes an interesting hook and clear claim while the conclusion neatly wraps up and supports the argument. Student uses transition words, phrases, or clauses to create a cohesive argument.	Student includes a clear introduction, body, and conclusion in the essay. The introduction includes an interesting hook and clear, concise claim while the conclusion neatly wraps up and supports the argument while adding a new and insightful way to look at the claim. Student creatively uses vivid and interesting transition words, phrases, or clauses to create a fluid, cohesive argument.
x1	Language Standards: 7.W.1d, 4; 7.L.1-3	Student's text is barely legible due to many grammar and spelling mistakes. Student fails to maintain a formal style.	Student has several grammar or spelling mistakes. Student attempts a formal style but still has several slang terms or personal pronouns.	Student uses correct grammar and spelling. Student mostly maintains a formal style throughout the text removing most slang and personal pronouns but might have missed a few.	Student uses correct grammar and spelling, choosing appropriate, interesting language (including any technical terminology from the text) to add variety to the text. Student maintains a formal style throughout the text, removing all slang and personal pronouns.	Student uses correct grammar and spelling. Student chooses appropriate, interesting language (including any technical terminology from the text) and factors in connotation and context in order to add variety, precision, and conciseness to the text. Student maintains a formal style throughout the text, removing all slang and personal pronouns.

Teacher Comments:

Name: _____ Class: _____ Date: _____

Informative Essay Rubric

Weight	Category	Incomplete 1	Minimally Proficient 2	Partially Proficient 3	Proficient 4	Highly Proficient 5
x1	Topic Standards: 7.W.2a, 4	The student does not have a clear topic/central idea nor any strategies to convey information. The essay reads like a confusing ramble.	Student attempts to introduce the topic/central idea but it is not specific or clear enough. Student attempts to use a strategy to convey information but does not make clear connections to the topic.	Student introduces the topic/central idea but may not include a preview of the essay. Student uses at least one strategy, such as definitions, classifications, comparisons/contrasts, or cause and effect to organize and convey information.	Student introduces the topic/central idea and a brief preview of the essay in the introduction. Student uses some combinations of strategies such as definitions, classifications, comparisons/contrasts, and/or cause and effect to organize and convey ideas, concepts, and information.	Student introduces the topic/central idea and a brief preview of the essay clearly and concisely in the introduction. Student uses many strategies such as definitions, classifications, comparisons/contrasts, and cause and effect to organize and effectively convey ideas, concepts, and information.
x2	Evidence Standards: 7.W.2b, 4	Claims presented are not supported with evidence.	Not all claims presented are supported with evidence. Evidence comes from sources that may or may not be credible or accurate and/or may not be correctly cited.	All claims presented are supported with evidence, including relevant facts, definitions, concrete details, or quotations. Evidence comes from accurate and credible sources but may not be correctly cited.	All claims presented are supported with relevant evidence, including some combination of relevant facts, definitions, concrete details, and/or quotations. Evidence comes from accurate and credible sources and is correctly cited.	All claims presented are supported with clear, strong, relevant evidence, including relevant facts, definitions, concrete details, and quotations. Evidence comes from accurate, credible, and interesting sources written by experts & is correctly cited.
x1	Organization Standards: 7.W.2c, 2f, 4	The essay has no clear structure or transitions between ideas.	Student includes an introduction, body, and conclusion in the essay but doesn't write complete paragraphs or sentences. The introduction may not include a claim while the conclusion may only consist of a generalities or filler sentences.	Student includes an introduction, body, and conclusion in the essay. The introduction includes a claim while the conclusion attempts to wrap up the essay by simply rephrasing or repeating the claim. Student attempts to use transition words, phrases, or clauses but essay might still feel choppy.	Student includes a clear introduction, body, and conclusion in the essay. The introduction includes an interesting hook and clear claim while the conclusion neatly wraps up and supports the essay. Student uses transition words, phrases, or clauses to create a cohesive argument.	Student includes a clear introduction, body, and conclusion in the essay. The introduction includes an interesting hook and clear, concise claim while the conclusion neatly wraps up and supports the essay while adding a new and insightful way to look at the claim. Student creatively uses vivid and interesting transition words, phrases, or clauses to create a fluid, cohesive argument.
x1	Language Standards: 7.W.2d, 2e, 4; 7.L.1-3	Student's text is barely legible due to many grammar and spelling mistakes. Student fails to maintain a formal style.	Student has several grammar or spelling mistakes. Student attempts a formal style but still has several slang terms or personal pronouns.	Student uses correct grammar and spelling. Student mostly maintains a formal style throughout the text removing most slang and personal pronouns but might have missed a few.	Student uses correct grammar and spelling, choosing appropriate, interesting language (including any technical terminology from the text) to add variety to the text. Student maintains a formal style throughout the text, removing all slang and personal pronouns.	Student uses correct grammar and spelling. Student chooses appropriate, interesting language (including any technical terminology from the text) & factors in connotation & context in order to add variety, precision, & conciseness to the text. Student maintains a formal style throughout the text, removing all slang and personal pronouns.

Thrown to the Wind Teacher's Resource   *Windy Sea Publishing, LLC*   www.windyseapublishing.com

Name: _____ Class: _____ Date: _____

Narrative Essay Rubric

Weight	Category	Incomplete 1	Minimally Proficient 2	Partially Proficient 3	Proficient 4	Highly Proficient 5
x1	Introduction Standards: 7.W.3a, 4	Student does not orient the reader or establish context.	Student attempts to orient the reader by establishing a context, setting, and POV but may have some unnecessary or missing details. Story progression feels choppy or unbelievable.	Student orients the reader by establishing a context, setting, and POV. Story progresses mostly believably from the introduction.	Student engages and orients the reader with an interesting opening line and quickly establishes a context, setting, and POV. Story progresses believably from the introduction.	Student engages and orients the reader with a captivating opening line and quickly and effectively establishes a context, setting, and POV. Story progresses naturally, surprisingly, and believably from the introduction.
x2	Narrative Standards: 7.W.3b, 4	Student does not use narrative techniques and/or they do not develop the story at all	Student uses few narrative techniques, such as dialogue, acing, and sensory descriptions, and/or they do not fully develop setting, character, or events.	Student uses some narrative techniques, such as dialogue, pacing, and sensory descriptions, to develop setting, events, and characters.	Student uses narrative techniques, such as dialogue, pacing, and sensory descriptions, to develop setting, events, and characters.	Student uses narrative techniques, such as interesting dialogue, exciting pacing, and vivid sensory descriptions, to develop immersive settings, engaging events, and relatable characters.
x1	Organization Standards: 7.W.3c, 3e, 4	The story has no clear structure or transitions between events and the story is confusing and/or does not include an introduction or conclusion.	Student includes an introduction, body, and conclusion in the story. The introduction may include a hook but does not have enough exposition to establish the story while the conclusion may not believably flow from the events of the story and/or the student may have rushed through the story, skipping important scenes. Student does not use many transitions.	Student includes an introduction, body, and conclusion in the story. The introduction includes a hook and some exposition while the conclusion wraps up the story in a way that is mostly believable. Student uses some transition words, phrases, or clauses to create a clear timeframe, setting and sequence of events.	Student includes a clear introduction, body, and conclusion in the story. The introduction includes an interesting hook and exposition while the conclusion neatly wraps up the story in a way that flows both naturally and believably from the events of the story. Student uses interesting transition words, phrases, or clauses to create a cohesive timeframe, setting and sequence of events.	Student includes a clear introduction, body, and conclusion in the story. The introduction includes an interesting hook and exposition while the conclusion neatly wraps up the story in a way that flows both naturally and surprisingly from the events of the story as well as with the characters' goals and motivations. Student creatively uses vivid and interesting transition words, phrases, or clauses to create a fluid, cohesive timeframe, setting and sequence of events.
x1	Language Standards: 7.W.3d, 4; 7.L.1-3	Student's text is barely legible due to many grammar and spelling mistakes.	Student has several grammar or spelling mistakes.	Student uses correct grammar and spelling.	Student uses correct grammar and spelling, choosing appropriate, interesting language (including any technical terminology from the text) to add variety to the text.	Student uses correct grammar and spelling. Student chooses applicable, interesting language (including any technical terminology from the text) and factors in connotation and context in order to add variety, precision, & conciseness to the text.

Teacher Comments:

Thrown to the Wind Teacher's Resource

Name: _____ Class: _____ Date: _____

Presentation Rubric

Weight	Category	Incomplete 1	Minimally Proficient 2	Partially Proficient 3	Proficient 4	Highly Proficient 5
x1	Preparation and Collaboration Standards: 7.SL.1a-d	Students do not come to discussions or the presentation prepared. The group squabbles and cannot get along or work together.	Some students come to group discussions prepared and/or the presentation, having read most materials and/or completing assigned tasks. Students attempt open discussion but there are a several heated or ineffective discussions. Students struggle to acknowledge new information or ideas expressed by others and/or struggle to find acceptable compromises. Students struggle to ask questions and/or answer questions posed by others. Students do not attempt to track progress and fall behind in their project.	Most students come to group discussions prepared and the presentation, having read all materials and/or completing assigned tasks. Students are open to discussion but there are a few ineffective or heated discussions. Students acknowledge new information or ideas expressed by others and are able to compromise though some students may still feel left out. Students are able to pose questions and answer questions posed by others. Students attempt to track progress but may miss specific deadlines or may not accomplish all goals.	All students come to all group discussions and the presentation prepared, having read all materials and/or completing assigned tasks. Students are open to discussion but there might be some easily resolved problems. Students acknowledge new information or ideas expressed by others and are able to form acceptable compromises. Students are able to pose questions and answer questions posed by others. Students track progress and keep specific goals and deadlines.	All students come to all group discussions and the presentation prepared, having read all materials and/or completing assigned tasks. Students are open to reasonable discussions without arguments. Students acknowledge new information or ideas expressed by others are able to create solutions/ideas that work for all. Students are able to pose thought-provoking questions and insightfully answer questions posed by others. Students effectively track progress and keep specific goals and deadlines.
x2	Content and Completion Standards: 7.SL.5; 7.L.1-3	Students do not have any visual elements to include.	Students have included visual displays in order to help make their points, but it is unfinished and/or messy and disorganized with many grammar mistakes.	Students have included visual displays in order to help make their points. There are few grammar mistakes made and most of the work has been completed.	Students have included interesting visual displays in order to help make their points. There are no grammar mistakes made and all work has been completed.	Students have included captivating and interesting visual displays in order to help make their points. There are no grammar mistakes made and all work has been completed a with high attention to detail.
x2	Presentation and Articulation Standards: 7.SL.4, 6; 7.L.3	Most or all of the students' claims and ideas are confusing. Most students are off task & unfocused. Students do not make good eye contact/or use an appropriate volume. There are many pronunciation errors and students sound monotone. There is no obvious organization, and no one knows who is supposed to speak.	Some of the students' claims and ideas are confusing. Several students are off task and unfocused. Students struggle to make good eye contact and/or use an appropriate volume. There are many pronunciation errors and students struggle to vary their tone. The presentation is poorly organized and/or the students do not know who is supposed to speak.	Students present their claims, findings, and ideas mostly coherently. Most students are on task and focused. Most students make good eye contact and use an appropriate volume. There are few pronunciation errors and students attempt to vary their tone in order to emphasize their important points. The presentation is mostly organized.	Students present their claims, findings, and ideas coherently. No student it off task or unfocused. Students make strong eye contact and use an appropriate volume. All words are clearly pronounced, and students vary their tone in order to emphasize salient points. The presentation is well organized.	Students present their claims, findings, & ideas coherently and engagingly. No student it off task or unfocused. All students make strong eye contact and use an appropriate volume that can be heard from anywhere in the room. All words are clearly and correctly pronounced, & students vary their tone and speech appropriately for the style of presentation in order to emphasize salient points and/or to create excitement/engagement with their listeners. Presentation is smooth and well organized.

Thrown to the Wind Teacher's Resource   *Windy Sea Publishing, LLC*   www.windyseapublishing.com

112

Name: _____ Class: _____ Date: _____

Research Project Rubric

Weight	Category	Incomplete 1	Minimally Proficient 2	Partially Proficient 3	Proficient 4	Highly Proficient 5
x1	Research Standards: 7.W.1a, 1b, 2a, 2b, 4-9	The student does not have a clear topic/central idea. Claims presented are not supported with evidence.	Student attempt to introduce the topic/central idea but it is not specific or clear enough. Not all claims presented are supported with evidence. Evidence comes from sources that may or may not be credible or accurate and/or may not be correctly cited.	Student introduces the topic/central idea but may not include a preview of the essay. All claims presented are supported with evidence, including relevant facts, definitions, concrete details, or quotations. Evidence comes from accurate and credible sources but may not be correctly cited.	Student introduces the topic/central idea and a brief preview of the essay in the introduction. All claims presented are supported with relevant evidence, including some combination of facts, definitions, concrete details, and/or quotations. Evidence comes from accurate and credible sources and is correctly cited.	Student introduces the topic/central idea and a brief preview of the essay clearly and concisely in the introduction. All claims presented are supported with clear, strong, and relevant evidence, including facts, definitions, concrete details, and quotations. Evidence comes from accurate, credible, and interesting sources written by experts and is correctly cited.
x2	Analysis Standards: 7.RI/RL.1-3, 5-9; 7.SL.2, 3	Student displays minimal or no understanding of the topic/central idea, text structure, author point of view and/or literary/technical elements of the text. Student cannot find any comparisons or contrasts between the texts and cannot trace the author's arguments. Student does not use evidence to support their explanation.	Student displays some understanding of the topic/central idea, text structure, author point of view and/or literary/technical elements of the text. Student is able to find simple comparisons and contrasts between most of the texts. Student struggles to trace arguments or specific claims in the texts but cannot assess their effectiveness. Student uses evidence, but it may be confusing or disconnected from their analysis.	Student displays a basic understanding of the topic/central idea, text structure, author point of view and/or literary/technical elements of the text. Student is able to find comparisons and contrasts between most of the texts. Student can trace arguments or specific claims in the texts but may struggle to assess their effectiveness. Student uses evidence, but it may not be the strongest example and/or may not clearly connect to their analysis.	All responses display a complete understanding of the topic/central idea, text structure, author point of view and/or literary/technical elements of the text. Student is able to find strong comparisons and contrasts between all the texts. Student can trace and evaluate arguments or specific claims in the texts and assess their effectiveness. Student uses relevant evidence and connects it to their analysis.	All responses display a complete, complex, and insightful understanding of the topics/central ideas, text structures, point of views, and/or literary/technical elements of all the texts. Student is able to find meaningful and insightful comparisons and contrasts between all the texts & to extrapolate the significance of them. Student can trace and evaluate arguments or specific claims in the texts and assess their effectiveness. Student chooses clear, strong, and relevant evidence and clearly connects it to their analysis.
	Organization Standards: 7.W.1c, 1e, 2c, 2f, 4; 7	The essay has no clear structure or transitions between ideas.	Student includes an introduction, body, and conclusion in the essay but doesn't write complete paragraphs or sentences. The introduction may not include a claim while the conclusion may only consist of a generalities or filler sentences.	Student includes an introduction, body, and conclusion in the essay. The introduction includes a claim while the conclusion attempts to wrap up the essay by simply rephrasing or repeating the claim. Student attempts to use transition words, phrases, or clauses but essay might still feel choppy.	Student includes a clear introduction, body, and conclusion in the essay. The introduction includes an interesting hook and clear claim while the conclusion neatly wraps up and supports the essay. Student uses transition words, phrases, or clauses to create a cohesive argument.	Student includes a clear introduction, body, and conclusion in the essay. The introduction includes an interesting hook and clear, concise claim while the conclusion neatly wraps up and supports the essay while adding a new and insightful way to look at the claim. Student creatively uses vivid and interesting transition words, phrases, or clauses to create a fluid, cohesive argument.

Thrown to the Wind Teacher's Resource   *Windy Sea Publishing, LLC*   www.windyseapublishing.com

x1	Language Standards: 7.RI/RL.4; 7.W.1d, 2d, 2e; 7.L.1-5	Student's text is barely legible due to many grammar and spelling mistakes. Student fails to maintain a formal style.	Student has several grammar or spelling mistakes. Student attempts a formal style but still has several slang terms or personal pronouns.	Student uses correct grammar and spelling. Student mostly maintains a formal style throughout the text removing most slang and personal pronouns but might have missed a few.	Student uses correct grammar and spelling, choosing appropriate, interesting language (including any technical terminology from the text) to add variety to the text. Student maintains a formal style throughout the text, removing all slang and personal pronouns.	Student uses correct grammar and spelling. Student chooses appropriate, interesting language (including any technical terminology from the text) & factors in connotation & context in order to add variety, precision, & conciseness to the text. Student maintains a formal style throughout the text, removing all slang and personal pronouns.
		For when students share research in a class discussion				
x1	Preparation and Collaboration Standards: 7.SL.1a-d	Students do not come to discussions or the presentation prepared. The group squabbles and cannot get along or work together.	Some students come to group discussions and/or the presentation prepared, having read most materials and/or completing assigned tasks. Students attempt open discussion, but several discussions are heated or ineffective. Students struggle to acknowledge new information or ideas expressed by others and/or struggle to find acceptable compromises. Students struggle to ask questions and/or answer questions posed by others. Students do not attempt to track progress and fall behind in their project.	Most students come to group discussions prepared for the presentation, having read all materials and/or completed assigned tasks. Students are open to discussion but there are a few ineffective discussions. Students acknowledge new information or ideas expressed by others and are able to compromise though some students may still feel left out. Students are able to pose questions & answer them from others. Students attempt to track progress but may miss specific deadlines or may not accomplish all goals.	All students come to all group discussions and the presentation prepared, having read all materials and/or completing assigned tasks. Students are open to discussion but there might be some easily resolved though heated discussions. Students acknowledge new information or ideas expressed by others and are able to form acceptable compromises. Students are able to pose questions and answer questions posed by others. Students track progress and keep specific goals and deadlines.	All students come to all group discussions and the presentation prepared, having read all materials and/or completing assigned tasks. Students are open to reasonable discussions without arguments. Students acknowledge new information or ideas expressed by others are able to create solutions/ideas that work for all. Students are able to pose thought-provoking questions and insightfully answer questions posed by others. Students effectively track progress and keep specific goals and deadlines.
		For when students present research as a group in front of the class				
x1	Presentation and Articulation Standards: 7.SL.4, 6; 7.L.3	Most or all of the students' claims and ideas are confusing. Most students are off task & unfocused. Students do not make good eye contact/or use an appropriate volume. There are many pronunciation errors and students sound monotone. There is no obvious organization, and no one knows who is supposed to speak.	Some of the students' claims and ideas are confusing. Several students are off task and unfocused. Students struggle to make good eye contact and/or use an appropriate volume. There are many pronunciation errors and students struggle to vary their tone. The presentation is poorly organized and/or the students do not know who is supposed to speak.	Students present their claims, findings, and ideas mostly coherently. Most students are on task and focused. Most students make good eye contact and use an appropriate volume. There are few pronunciation errors and students attempt to vary their tone in order to emphasize their important points. The presentation is mostly organized.	Students present their claims, findings, and ideas coherently. No student it off task or unfocused. Students make strong eye contact and use an appropriate volume. All words are clearly pronounced, and students vary their tone in order to emphasize salient points. The presentation is well organized.	Students present their claims, findings, and ideas coherently and engagingly. No student it off task or unfocused. All students make strong eye contact and use an appropriate volume that can be heard from anywhere in the room. All words are clearly and correctly pronounced, and students vary their tone and speech appropriately for the style of presentation in order to emphasize salient points and/or to create excitement/engagement with their listeners. Presentation is smooth and well organized.

Appendix B
Additional Sources

Duane A. Cline, ***The Pilgrims and Plymouth Colony: 1620***, 1999.
   http://sites.rootsweb.com/~mosmd/index.htm#part2

   This site has an incredible amount of information for teachers and students, not just on the Pilgrims and Plymouth Colony, but also on sailing and navigational tools. He includes numerous student activities for creating and using the navigational tools of the 17th century. These include creating:

   - Sandglasses
   - Mariner's Magnetic Compass
   - The Back-Staff
   - The Astrolabe
   - The Nocturnal
   - The Mariner's Quadrant
   - The Traverse Board
   - The Compass Rose
   - The Log-Line
   - The Hand Lead-Line
   - The Cross Staff

Smithsonian, "Time and Navigation: The Untold Story of Getting from Here to There"
   https://timeandnavigation.si.edu

   This site has a lot of information for students and teachers, including navigating at sea, in the air and in space, satellite navigation, a timeline of innovation, and videos explaining how latitude and longitude and GPS work.

Vanderhoof Family History Project
   http://www.vanderhoofproject.com/index.php/the-journey/more-about-de-bever

   This site has the original Journal of De Bever, 1661 both in Dutch and English along with passenger lists, including the amounts of money owed by those who indentured themselves to take the voyage, letters from the WIC Directors to Peter Stuyvesant, maps, and other genealogical information.

Elford Eddy, ***The Log of a Cabin Boy***, 1922
   https://books.google.com/books?id=Jug7AQAAMAAJ&printsec=frontcover&source=gbs_ge_summary_r&cad=0#v=onepage&q&f=false

   This book is available as a free ebook on Google Books and can be downloaded as a pdf.

Richard's Dystopian Pokeverse, "Dutch Ships in the 17th Century: a diorama for CCH"
   https://lurkerablog.wordpress.com/2013/12/09/dutch-ships-in-the-17th-century-a-diorama-for-cch/

   This website contains information on Texel Harbor in the Netherlands, along with maps and beautiful images of dioramas showing what the harbor would have looked like in the 17th century. He also includes maps and images of Amsterdam.

Marcus Flynn, ***Pyromasse***, "Les Potagers"
   https://www.pyromasse.ca/articles/potager_e.html

   This website provides information and many photographs and diagrams of the 17th century French stoves discussed in *Thrown to the Wind*.

Appendix C
Sources Cited for Thrown to the Wind

Family Histories and Genealogies

Griffin, Judy. *Gano Family*, 2007.

Gunnoe, Judith. The Gunnoe Family of West Virginia, 5/25/2013.

Hervey, Robert. "Early Gano History," *Hervey Family History, 2001*. Lineage Online.

Lemaster, Howard Marshall. *Gano Family, U.S.A., 1970*. Carlinville, IL, 1970.

Huguenots and France, History and Theology

Baird, Charles W. *History of the Huguenot Emigration to America*. New York, NY: Dodd, Mead & Company Publishers, 1885.

This is an excellent history of the French Huguenots and the reasons they left France for Holland, England, and eventually, America. It discusses the challenges they faced in the New World.

Bertolet, Tim. "Calvin's Theology: Predestination," *Place for Truth*. September 20, 2017. Web.

Cole, Henry, Translator. John Calvin, *Calvin's Calvinsim: Treatises on the Eternal Predestination of God and the Secret Providence of God*. Grand Rapids, Michigan: Reformed Free Publishing Association, n.d.

DeLisio, Phyllis and Rose Stella Proscia. *S1350 and the Memorial Church of the Huguenots*. Reformed Church of Huguenot Park, nd. Web.
This history of the founding of the Huguenot church and settlement on Staten Island in 1661 is well footnoted and gives valuable insight into this period.

Flynn, Marcus. "Les Potagers," *Pyromasse*. Montreal, Canada: 2009.

This article provided numerous images and descriptions of the French potager stoves, like the ones built by Etienne Gayneau, Sr.

Journael of De Bever July – May 1661 Translation. New York Historical Society, Vanderhoof Project, 2012.

The original document *'Journael Behouden opt'schip den Gulden Bever en t'schip den Gulden Otter'* is held by the New York Historical Society; Ref MSS.Ships.Journals.1600/Ships Collection Box 1 Folder #34 and a transcript of the original is included as Appendix A. The Journal contains descriptions of four voyages based on notes by an unknown author, probably an employee of the Dutch West India Company. The first voyage is the one of interest here as it details the voyage on which the Gayneau Family traveled from Holland to New Amsterdam in 1661.

La Rocca, Donald J. *The Academy of the Sword: Illustrated Fencing Books 1500-1800*. New York: The Metropolitan Museum of Art, 1998.

This was a valuable resource for showing the 17th century French blade weapons and styles of fencing at the time. It includes numerous images.

The Huguenot Fellowship Historical Blogs.

"The Siege of La Rochelle," *The Baldwin Project* taken from *The Story of France*, by Mary Macgregor. New York: Frederick A. Stokes Company, 1911, which is now in the public domaine.

"The Edict of Nantes (1598)" *The 16th Century*. Museeprotestant, France: n.d. Accessed 10/27/2018.

"The period of the Revocation of the Edict of Nantes (1661-1700)," *The 17th Century*. Museeprotestant, France: n.d. Accessed 10/27/2018.

This site was invaluable in providing the timeline and history of the Huguenot persecution in France. It detailed the policies of King Louis XIV that provided the necessary background and filled in the details leading to the Gayneau's flight from La Rochelle in 1660.

Von Goeth, Aurora. "The Art of Addressing French Nobility," *Party Like 1660.*, 2015-2019.

Images (In order of appearance)

Van de Velde the Younger, Willem. *A Ship on the High Seas Caught by a Squall*, known as *"The Gust"* (1680), Rijksmuseum, Amsterdam. Used with permission. Appears on the cover.

1814 Thomson Map of the Atlantic Ocean. Public Domain.

Western Europe in year 1700 "Courtesy of the University of Texas Libraries, The University of Texas at Austin." Accessed 12/7/18.

"The trip from Texel to Staten Island Begin: The first leg of the trip," The Vanderhoof Family History Project. Accessed 12/7/18.

"The Second Let of the Trip," The Vanderhoof Family History Project. Accessed 12/7/18.

"The Third Leg of the Trip," The Vanderhoof Family Project. Accessed 12/7/18.

Corot, Jean Baptist Camille. *La Rochelle, The Harbour Entrance*, The Yorck Project (2002) *10.000 Meisterwerke der Malerei* (DVD-ROM), distributed by DIRECTMEDIA Publishing GmbH. ISBN: 3936122202.

Vroom, Hendrick Cornelisz. *Return to Amsterdam of the Second Expedition to the East Indies* (1599), Rijksmuseum, Amsterdam. Used with permission.

Flynn, Marcus. "The Potager's Stove," *Les Potegers*. Used with permission.

Gunter, Edmund. "Navigation: an astrolabe, a cross-staff, and a back-staff or Davis's sextant." Drawing, 1624. Rights: Welcome Collection, CC BY 4.0. Converted to black and white and labeled. Used with permission. http://creativecommons.org/licenses/by/4.0/

Vroom, Hendrick Cornelisz. *De Vergulde Bever (The Gilded Beaver)* (1660), Rijksmuseum, Amsterdam. Used with permission.

Tantillo, Len. *Manhattan 1660*. Used with permission.

New York (New Netherlands) Colony

Cohen, Paul E. and Robert T. Augustyn. *Manhattan in Maps: 1527-1995.* New York, New York: Rizzoli International Publications, Inc., 1997. Web.

> In addition to providing a large number of historic maps of Manhattan, this book also provides a thorough history of Manhattan from early colonization to the twentieth century.

Elson, Henry William and Kathy Leigh, translator. "New Amsterdam," *History of the United States.* New York: MacMillan Company, 1904. Web.

> This well-footnoted history of the colony of New Amsterdam is a good general history of the colony.

Gardiner, Jonathan T., Jonathan Baker, Joseph S. Osborn, Eds. *Records of the Town of East-Hampton, Long Island, Suffolk Co., N.Y., with Other Ancient Documents of Historic Value.*, Vol. 1. SAG-Harbor, N.Y.: John H. Hunt, Printer, 1887.

Leng, Charles W., B.Sc. and William T. Davis. *Staten Island and Its People: A History 1609 – 1929*, Vols. 1-2, New York, NY: Lewis Historical Publishing Company, Inc. 1930.

Matteo, Thomas. "Staten Island Brief History," *The Staten Island Historian.* Staten Island, NY: Rhinostudio.com, 2008-2012. Web.

Ricker, James. Revised History of Harlem (City of New York): Its Origin and Early Annals: Perfaced by Homes Scenes in the Fatherlands; Or Notices of Its Founders Before Emigration. Also, Sketches of Numerous Families, and the Recovered History of the Land-Titles …. New York, NY: New Harlem Publishing Company, 1904.

Staten Island Advance. *History: A Timeline of Staten Island.* SILive.com, 2014. Web.

Sublett, John, Louis. *Staten Island Folklore.* Amazon Digital Services, Inc., June 1, 2011. Kindle Book.

Sublett, John Louis. *Staten Island: A Walk Down Memory Lane.* CreateSpace, January 28, 2009. Kindle Book.

> This book provides a convenient timeline of important events affecting Staten Island and some information on prominent people associated with the island. It also provides a valuable listing of books on Staten Island.

Sailing and Maritime History

Anderson, R. C. *The Rigging of Ships in the Days of the Spritsail Topmast, 1600-1720.* New York, New York: Dover Publications, Inc., 1927. Print.

> This is an excellent resource for researching the technical details of rigging a variety of English,

Dutch, French, Portuguese, and Spanish ships during the indicated time period. There is also a useful illustration of the English Merchantman, 1673.

Culver, Henry B. *The Book of Old Ships From Egyptian Galleys to Clipper Ships.* New York, New York: Dover Publications, Inc., 1992. Print.

This book contains 81 illustrations of different types of ships and descriptions of them and their uses.

Exquemelin, Alexander O. and Alexis Brown, Translator. *The Buccaneers of America.* Mineola, New York: Dover Publications, Inc., 1969. Print.

The book discusses the English, French, and Dutch buccaneers of the Caribbean.

Jeans, Peter D. *Seafaring Lore & Legend: A Miscellany of Maritime Myth, Superstition, Fable, and Fact.* International Marine/ McGraw Hill, 2004. Print.

This book also includes maritime history, nautical customs, descriptions of life at sea, information on the Press Gang and types of ships.

Lavery, Brian. *Ship: The Epic Story of Maritime Adventure.* New York, New York: DK Publishing, Inc., 2008. Print.

This is a good general resource with a wealth of visual images.

Paine, Ralph D. *The Old Merchant Marine: A Chronicle of American Ships and Sailors.* iBooks, n.d.

This book is well researched, including a detailed and lengthy annotated bibliography.

Additional Sources for Teacher's Resource
"1637 Tulipmania," *Timeline Dutch History – Rijksstudio*, (Rijksmuseum).

A Timeline of North American Exploration, 1492-1585, (ThoughtCo).

Bayers, Johann. "An Engraving of Orion," *Uranometria*, 1603. US Navel Observatory Library.

Blok, Petrus Johannes, *History of the people of the Netherlands* (New York: G. P. Putnam's Sons, 1898).

Boxer, Charles R., *The Dutch in Brazil 1624 - 1654.* (Oxford, Clarendon Press, 1957).

Boxer, Charles R., *The Dutch Seaborne Empire 1600–1800,* (Oxford, Clarendon Press, 1965).

Catechism of the Catholic Church, no.882.

CE Editors, *Explaining the Hierarchy of the Church.* Catholic Exchange. Feb. 17th, 2005.

Celebrating Christmas, (Presbyterian Heritage Center, 2011).

dal Covolo, Fr. Enrico, S.D.B, The Historical Origin of Indulgences, (Catholic Culture, 2019).

Danko, C. "Once Upon a Time When Christmas Was Banned ...", *A Puritan's Mind*, (Puritans Publications, 1996-2019).

Flesher, Paul, *Banned Christmas*, (Religion Today, 12/7/2010).

French Court Etiquette at Versailles and Who Was "Madame Etiquette"?, "Etiquipedia", (Friday, Dec. 20, 2013).

Haley, Kenneth, Harold, Dobson, *The Dutch in the Seventeenth Century. Thames and Hudson* (Oxford University Press, 1972), p. 78.

Hayden, J. Michael and Malcolm R. Greenshields, *French Historical Studies*: "The Clergy of Early Seventeenth Century France: Self-Perception and Society's Perception." Vol. 18, No. 1 (Spring, 1993), pp. 145-172

Israel, Jonathan Irvine, *The Dutch Republic: Its Rise, Greatness, and Fall 1477-1806*, (1995).

Janda, Setareh, *Royal French Manners Were so Weird that You Could Pee Directly in Front of the Queen*, "Weird History".

Johann Tetzel, (Encylopaedia Britannica, 2007).

Jonker, Joost, *Merchants, bankers, middlemen: the Amsterdam money market during the first half of the 19th century*, (NEHA, 1996), p. 32.

Lane, Kris E., *Pillaging the Empire: Piracy in the Americas 1500-1750*, (M. E. Sharpe, 1998).l;'

Macgregor, Mary. "The Siege of La Rochelle," *The Story of France*, by Mary Macgregor. *The Baldwin Project.* (New York: Frederick A. Stokes Company, 1911).

Peters, Edward, *A Modern Guide to Indulgences: Rediscovering this Often Misinterpreted Teaching*, (Chicago: Hillenbrand Books, 2008), 13.

Pike, John, *"Nobility - Classes and Precedence,"* (Global Security org, 2011).

Raad van Adel, Hoge (in Dutch), "Adeldom: Predikaat of Title," (Archived from the original on 23 April 2015. Retrieved 5 May 2015).

Reynolds, John Mark, *Ten Reasons for Calvinists to Be Cheerful this Christmas*, (First Things, 12/5/09)

Rowen, Herbert H, *The princes of Orange: the stadtholders in the Dutch Republic*, (Cambridge University Press, 1988), p.29.

Stilwell, James Joseph and James E. Vance, *Ship*, "History of Ships", (Encyclopedia Britanica, Inc., June 22, 2018).

Temple, Sir William, *Observations upon the United Provinces of the Netherlands (7th ed.)*, "London: Jacob Tonfon within Grays-Inn Gate next Grays-Inn Lane, and Awnfoam and John Churchill at the Black Swan in Tater-No/ler-Row."

"The Edict of Nantes (1598)," *The 16th Century*. Museeprotestant, (France: n.d. Accessed 10/27/2018).

"The Period of the Revocation of the Edict of Nantes (1661-1700)," *The 17th Century*. (Museeprotestant, France: n.d. Accessed 10/27/2018).

Walton, Timothy R. *The Spanish Treasure Fleets,* (Pineapple Press Inc, 2002), p. 57.